PENGUIN BOOKS

MAD ABOUT CUBA

Ullekh N.P. is an author, journalist, columnist and political commentator based in New Delhi and Kerala. A bilingual writer and public speaker, his earlier books are *Kannur: Inside India's Bloodiest Revenge Politics* (2018), *The Untold Vajpayee: Politician and Paradox* (2016) and *War Room: The People, Tactics and Technology Behind Narendra Modi's 2014 Win* (2015). He is the subject of episode 1 of the documentary web series *Love Storiyaan* (2024) on Amazon Prime.

'Ullekh N.P. takes us on an enchanting journey from his childhood in Kerala, an Indian state distinguished by a fascination with Cuba, Fidel Castro and Che Guevara, to contemporary Cuba. From the peaceful green lawns of the Hotel National, he rides a classic car through the restaurants and bars of Havana and visits the famous tobacco fields of Pinar del Río where he learns how to roll a cigar. On the way, he speaks to scientists, government officials, taxi drivers and street sellers, intertwining his observations with historical background and political analysis to capture the complexity, contradictions and achievements of Cuban development since the Revolution of 1959. And inevitably, we hear about the pervasive presence of the US blockade. Beyond that, the author provides a fascinating perspective of the bonds between Cuba and Kerala, from political commitments to culinary tastes and the climate'—**Dr Helen Yaffe, senior lecturer, University of Glasgow, and author of *We Are Cuba!: How a Revolutionary People Have Survived in a Post-Soviet World* and *Che Guevara: The Economics of Revolution***

MAD ABOUT
CUBA

A MALAYALI REVISITS THE REVOLUTION

ULLEKH N.P.

PENGUIN BOOKS

An imprint of Penguin Random House

PENGUIN BOOKS

Penguin Books is an imprint of the Penguin Random House group of companies whose addresses can be found at global.penguinrandomhouse.com

Published by Penguin Random House India Pvt. Ltd
4th Floor, Capital Tower 1, MG Road,
Gurugram 122 002, Haryana, India

Penguin
Random House
India

First published in Penguin Books by Penguin Random House India 2024

ISBN 9780143469018

Typeset in Minion Pro by MAP Systems, Bengaluru, India
Printed at Replika Press Pvt. Ltd, India

www.penguin.co.in

MIX
Paper | Supporting
responsible forestry
FSC™ C016779

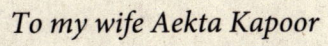

To my wife Aekta Kapoor

Contents

The Barwoman of Vedado

I met Enrique for the second time at Havana's Plaza de la Revolucion where he took two selfies of us, one with a large frame of Che Guevara and another with that of Camilo Cienfuegos in the background.

We knew each other from the hotel, although we had never talked. The Dominican tourist and I had bought almost the same set of books on the Cuban Revolution from the hotel bookshop. He had purchased the Spanish editions and I the English ones. Standing in the queue to pay up, we had exchanged warm smiles. In my home state of Kerala, which falls in the southern part of India and where we speak Malayalam, we describe such an instant affinity for each other with the phrase, *raktham rakthathe thiricharinju* (loosely translated as 'blood recognizes blood').

When we met again, he surmised rightly that I was politically in love with Cuba just as he was. Cubans would call the likes of him *toro*, a strong man, because of his squat gym physique. He gave me an odd piece of advice, nothing to do with politics: that the best way to enjoy evenings in Havana was to stay put in the hotel, listen to music by regular performers, dance with them and drink white rum late into the night. Go out only during the day, he said in a low voice. He did not explain his reasoning and I never got the opportunity again to ask why.

Enrique went on to tell me in broken English that he recommended another 'hidden pleasure'—gazing at the Malecon, Havana's iconic beachfront with its out-of-the-world curved corniche road, from the lawns of the Nacional de Cuba Hotel where I was staying, smoking a cigar if I liked doing so, all alone. 'Hidden pleasure,' he repeated before he introduced his family to me, hugged me tightly in the way of soul-brothers and said goodbye with a loud laugh and a slogan made famous worldwide by Fidel Castro and Che Guevara: 'Patria o Muerte' (Homeland or Death).

In tourist spots, the most frequent tip you get from fellow tourists and locals alike is that the 'real' fun is outside of the hotel. Enrique's was the opposite. It was a strange proposition. Why did he say that?

To find out, I took a break that night from the city's bars and restaurants made famous by Ernest Hemingway and many others, and decided to spend time on my hotel premises. Hemingway, I had found out, had been to Nacional de Cuba Hotel, but it was not one of his much-advertised haunts. Other luminaries who had stayed here include John Wayne, Frank Sinatra, Nat King Cole, Ava Gardner and Winston Churchill.

The band here appeared to have a clear directive: to play songs that made people dance and feel happy, so I jived in front of them sportingly. Later, I handed them a few dollars and retreated to the semi-open bar on the lawns that Enrique had recommended.

There were hardly any servers in the bar. After failing to catch their attention with my hands, eyes, and a few 'excuse me's . . .' that blew away in the wind, I was now staring at people walking by the well-lit part of the Malecon far below. As the largest island in the Caribbean Sea, Cuba is breathtakingly beautiful and a magnet for tourists with its shimmering blue sea, stately mountains, colonial architecture, old-world charm, iconic cocktails, addictive music and the innocent faces of its people.

My eyes travelled to the edge of the lawn where cannons named Krupp and Ordonez stood their ground. One of them had fired upon the USS Montgomery, a cruiser, during the Spanish-American War of 1898.[*] I could barely make out the people down there, young men and women who looked like dots from my seat, which felt like a throne, but their happiness was palpable.

Why were they out there this late?

Cubans look weary during the day when they commute back and forth from home and office in crowded, run-down *guagua*[†] buses that come after long waits, and so it was pleasant to see them cheerful now.[‡]

---

[*] The hotel, constructed atop the site of the eighteenth-century Santa Clara Battery, had served as Fidel Castro's headquarters for aerial defence during the Cuban Missile Crisis of 1962.

[†] The guagua is the form of bus transport used by most Cubans.

[‡] Havana is the only city in the country that has affordable public bus services. The other provinces depend on colectivos (shared taxis), trucks, the kindness of the people who have a company car, or company buses to go from one part of town to the other.

I watched the seafront for a very long time before I decided to place my order. Withdrawing my glance from the vastness of the ocean at nighttime, I waved at one of the two barwomen behind the counter.

The younger of the two walked up to me. 'What do you want?' she asked with great warmth.

'Bourbon with soda and ice,' I responded. Bourbon for me is like white rum for Enrique, I smiled to myself.

She was gone like an even-toed antelope.

It was 2 a.m. Crossing the Malecon, strong winds from the Gulf of Mexico swept into the Nacional de Cuba Hotel, suggesting that it was a good idea to stay awake. This isn't the time to retire to your suite, they seemed to say, but to relish the sound and feel of the sea breeze caressing your skin. Or that was how I interpreted it.

I felt hungry.

When the server returned, I told her that I wanted to order a few slices of bread and butter. 'Shall I show you the menu?' she asked. Eating meat and fish late at night didn't suit me—I was about to tell her that was why I chose bread and butter. But she was gone again like an antelope.

I ate like a savage without any table etiquette, like an American Bully XL that was starved for three days or more. To my great amusement, she had also served banana chips—god, this tastes slightly different compared with those in Kerala, where the signature gift item for outsiders is banana chips of all varieties.

The two servers had found seats behind the bar counter to rest and the cashier was snoring away in his seat. His spectacles were about to fall off, but they didn't. Certain acts in life defy gravity. His spectacles didn't fall even when he was woken up by the only customer left in the bar other than me who was in a sudden hurry to pay the bill and leave.

Exactly half an hour later, I waved again and ordered a refill. I didn't have to shout, 'Excuse me?'—she was looking at me curiously from behind the counter. This time, she didn't leave but stood there at a modest distance. I asked her where she stayed in the city. She went on to narrate the story of her life—of the past twenty or so years. Born in Santiago de Cuba, a city more than 850 kilometres from Havana, her parents moved to the Cuban capital when she was just three because she had a paediatric health condition that could only be treated at the capital. Her mother was a doctor and her father a cabbie. She studied English at Havana University. 'Do you know? Of my classmates who finished studies last December, only five of us are still here. Others have all left.'

'Where have they gone?' I questioned.

'To the US and Spain mostly, looking for jobs. People are leaving the country in large numbers,' she replied.

I told her that I was born in Kerala and that we grew up inspired by the Cuban Revolution that brought Fidel Castro and his fellow revolutionaries to power. I told her stories about the Revolution that I had read in Malayalam translations of books by Castro and his comrade-in-arms Che Guevara and in English by the likes of Gabriel Garcia Marquez and Eduardo Galeano, both great friends of Cuba. She was not familiar with many of my stories except about Castro and his lifelong fight against the might of the Americans. Then I switched my focus to the US. I blamed the US for the blockade, which the Americans call 'embargo', against Cuba, the characterization of her small country as a terrorist state, and dished out a few bits of jargon from political theory to explain why the American sanctions are essentially global sanctions.

'The Americans have always wanted existing power structures in Cuba to fall. They wanted to turn this country into what it was: their entertainment destination, a spot where they could do anything that was illegal in the US, a place where before 1958 anything was possible, a haven for gambling, drugs and prostitution that it was. Have you read the book, *The Mafia in Havana* by Enrique Cirules? American gangsters ruled this place until Fidel came to power. Did you know that this very hotel was the headquarters of the American mafia? Have you heard of Lucky Luciano? Have you watched the scene in *Godfather II* where Michael meets an organized crime figure named Hyman Roth, whose character is based on the life of American mobster Meyer Lansky? It happened here on the second floor (Hotel Nacional de Cuba) of . . .'*

I was definitely talking a lot.

She interjected, holding her hands in such a way as though to suggest 'my turn', and launched into a monologue without pause. 'Our leaders are blaming the American sanctions, but we young people have no interest in reasons, we want results, we want to live like people we find on Instagram and on Twitter, we have studied hard and worked hard, my mother works all the time, but she earns a pittance,

---

* Although the incident is shown as having occurred in Havana's Nacional Hotel, the 1974 film was actually shot in the Dominican Republic, which was passed off as Cuba.

5000 pesos a month, my father earns much more, but that is their generation who is interested in the Utopia of the Revolution, we are not. We want to live life well, we think life can be easy, life must be easy, we don't want to wait for rations and always worry about what we eat and what we cannot eat, we want to go out and order a burger, we want to travel and earn the money to travel the world, we don't want to live like this confined to the city. We see so many people come here and enjoy life and spend money. We see them spend loads of money and we don't want to live underpaid like our parents because we don't have their commitment, and we don't think it is needed. Our life is our life, I tell you, life is easy for you, isn't it? Then it must be easy for me too.'

She was still not breathless.

After we both ran out of words, I walked to the counter along with her in silence, paid with my credit card, and on the way back, handed her a twenty-dollar bill before heading back to the room. A sudden rise in humidity made me sweat, and I was worried about whether housekeeping had stocked up my fridge—or I would have to wake them up and wait for water. I felt dehydrated by the weight of history, its tragedy, its fatigue of racing against time and the onslaught of modernity.

I rushed to my room from where I could see the bar from my window. I surveyed the bar while gulping water directly from a big bottle I found in my room. The young barwoman was gone. The cashier was asleep with his specs hanging from his face in a precarious fashion. The older lady was smoking away furiously.

Enrique, I am sure, had a vastly different experience.

Faraway, in the Malecon, the dots were gone. So were the stars that reminded me of the dreams of the Revolution of 1959. The wind had stopped blowing and, like in the movies, the Cuban flag fluttered in slow motion.

My thoughts wandered.

Reading Fidel in Malayalam

The word 'Cuba' is part of my earliest memories. I came across the name Fidel Castro (not quite like how the Americans pronounce it, but something that sounded more like 'Fidhal Kaastro', rather like how Karl Marx was 'Kaaral Marx') for the first time in a newspaper in Malayalam, my mother tongue. Which is to say, I had heard the name 'Fidel' much before world politics became part of my mind's lexicon. The year was 1982 and I was in primary school. All of a sudden, he was being widely discussed among the elders in our Marxist household in Kannur, a northern district of Kerala.

Kerala, in southern India, flaunts a special history: it was here that the Communist Party of India (CPI) was voted to power in an election in 1957. It was a first for Asia and, besides San Marino (a microstate enclaved by Italy) and British Guyana (located in South America), it was the third communist government to be formally elected. As they say in Malayalam, *Kerala manassu edathu manassu* (The Kerala mind is a leftist mind). The influence of leftist politics in Kerala was so deep that it spawned a literary culture that familiarized the people with classics and heroes associated with liberation movements from afar. From Francis

Fanon's *The Wretched of the Earth* and Julius Fučík's *Notes from the Gallows* to Ethel Lilian Voynich's *The Gadfly* (all works translated into Malayalam), books were lapped up by those under the spell of the romance of the Revolution. Alongside, high literacy rates ensured an above-average interest in world politics. A combination of all these made Castro a recognizable name in the state. Castro, at that time in my childhood, was in the news over his comments about the war in the Falkland Islands, which the military junta of the time in Argentina decided to occupy by force, prompting a war with the British, who claimed that the islands southeast of Argentina—and 8000 miles away from England—were theirs.

Castro made an unlikely statement in Argentina's favour more than a month after Britain launched the war, although the right-wing junta in power in the Latin American nation was backed by Cuba's archenemy, the United States. Cuba had been silent and its communist ally, the Soviet Union, ambivalent for weeks. Perhaps sensing that Britain was winning the war, Castro called upon non-aligned nations (those part of the Non-Aligned Movement) to take 'whatever steps you may seem appropriate' to 'stop the British-US aggression'.[1]

The Americans who had initially tried to negotiate a peace deal for their Latin American ally later threw their weight behind the UK, their NATO ally from Europe, when it became clear that the Argentine regime was in no mood to relent. Its leaders used the occasion to distract the public from the excesses of the 'Dirty War' (which started in 1976 and would end in 1983) against suspected leftist political opponents during the course of which up to 30,000 citizens were killed or made to disappear. Obviously, the reason why Castro lashed out against the NATO forces had more to do with the existential threat his country faced from the US rather than politics in Argentina.

After this event, I did not hear about Castro until 1983, when he was covered extensively in India as the man who bear-hugged the then Prime Minister Indira Gandhi at the inauguration of the Non-Aligned Summit in New Delhi, which was attended by more than a hundred heads of state. At a time when Indian women, especially those in positions of power, were not photographed hugging men, certainly not those unrelated to them, the incident at Delhi's Vigyan Bhavan created a stir and sensation—and left Mrs Gandhi blushing. A dashing man with a beard and film-star looks, and more than that, charisma—for us kids, his photographs in dailies left a lasting impression.

I would read later from the account of the veteran career diplomat K. Natwar Singh, a Congress leader and an associate of Mrs Gandhi, that it was at this summit that Castro introduced Mrs Gandhi to someone admired by the world and idolized by us Malayalis: Gabriel Garcia Marquez, the Bogota-born Nobel Prize-winning writer. The Castro–Marquez friendship had elicited considerable interest in the Colombian literary genius, whose position on Cuba made him unpopular among some other contemporary writers like the Peruvian writer, Mario Vargas Llosa, who attacked Marquez using an expression that translated to 'courtesan of Cuba'. Although I love Llosa, I believe he was being grossly harsh to his former friend.

In sharp contrast, in Kerala, Marquez's support for Cuba only added to the unending mystique around him. He even wrote a non-fiction work titled *Images of Cuba,* in which he talks about various events in Cuba's history in the first decades since the 1959 Revolution. Some excerpts from that work were included in *The Strange Pilgrims,* a collection of short stories he had written over a long period. That book was translated into Malayalam, along with a few other important works of his, and is widely appreciated.

Marquez became one of my favourite authors ever since I first read him in Malayalam in 1990. His Cuban link did make him more popular in the state—and surprisingly it didn't make him unpopular even among those who disagreed with his political views. The first Marquez book I read was the translation of *One Hundred Years of Solitude* (*Ekanthathayude Nooru Varshangal* in Malayalam). He also became the favourite of publishers and booksellers in the state. Malayali publisher Ravi D.C., who runs Kerala's top publishing house DC Books, had this to say about Marquez in an interview shortly after his passing away in 2014, 'Marquez has been accepted and enjoyed by Keralites as a Malayali writer and not as a foreigner. We first published Marquez in Malayalam in the early 1980s and he continues to be a best-seller.'[2]

Journalist and Marquez buff K.P.M. Basheer wrote shortly after the literary icon's demise, 'The Malayali's fixation with Marquez, which began in the 1970s, is best told in these jokes: Marquez is "the best known Malayali writer in Latin America" and the "first Malayalam author who has won the Nobel".'[3] In recognition of his fanbase in the state, Malayali novelist-short story writer N.S. Madhavan, a former civil servant and leftist political commentator, proclaimed in jest that 'Marquez is a Malayali'. In February 2023, when the *Mathrubhumi Daily* organized its annual literature festival in the state capital Thiruvananthapuram, one of the participants was Marquez's grandson Mateo García Elizondo. I met him at the festival, which was curated by my friend and classmate Sabin Iqbal, and found Mateo overwhelmed by how much we Malayalis knew about his grandfather. Following my advice, he paid a visit to the Modern Book Centre, one of the finest booksellers in the state from where we used to purchase his grandfather's books in our college days in the mid-1990s.

Kerala is not just known for its fascination with the books of Marquez, the great lover of Cuba, but also for its romantic notion of communism that flowered with the success of the Cuban Revolution. It was in that left politics-effervescent climate of 1980s Kerala that I read the Malayalam translation of *Fidel & Religion: Conversations with Frei Betto on Marxism & Liberation Theology*. I was in high school then. The title in the Malayalam translation by C.P. Narayanan was *Fidel Castro Mathathe Patti* (Fidel Castro on Religion).[4] The book features a conversation between Castro and the Brazilian Dominican friar Frei Betto on Christianity, his school days, and the revolution. The sheer pleasure of reading this inspired me to later re-read the work in English. In their chat, Castro told Betto about meeting a delegation of US bishops, 'I told them that if they organized a state in accord with Christian precepts, they'd create one similar to ours.' On the other hand, Castro regretted that in practice, the Catholic Church had been used more for doing evil than good. He had also famously noted, 'I believe Karl Marx could have subscribed to the Sermon on the Mount as a tool for domination, exploitation and oppression for centuries.'[5] By saying so, Castro was trying to project a certain convergence between Marx's views and the sayings of Jesus (picked up from the Gospel of Mathew) as evident from the latter's call to stand up for the destitute and marginalized. Nothing else was a more overriding concern for Marx than the emancipation of the poor, the working class.

Another of Castro's works that the political left in Kerala was exposed to was *Charithram Enne Kuttakkaranallennu Vidhikkum* (the Malayalam translation of his two-hour speech on 16 October 1953 titled 'History Will Absolve Me'). The speech was made in his own defence against the charges levelled against him for leading the attack on the Moncada Barracks on 26 July 1953 in Santiago de Cuba as part of a movement to unseat what he described as the misrule of Fulgencio Batista, the Cuban dictator of the time. The young

Castro said in his speech that the Batista regime, '… merely brought with it a change of hands and a redistribution of the loot among a new group of friends, relatives, accomplices and parasitic hangers-on that constitute the political retinue of the Dictator.'[6] The impact of that defiant speech on me, although much would have been lost in translation from Spanish to English and then to Malayalam, was electrifying, to say the least. Castro, born in 1926 and trained as a lawyer, was just twenty-six at the time. Some of us friends, all of us like-minded and curious about Cuba, also shared books on Castro and discussed them along with works on and by the Argentine-born Cuban revolutionary, Che Guevara, a friend of Castro's who was even more left-leaning than Castro himself.

I was also forever quizzing my paternal uncle, Pattiam Rajan, a former member of the Indian Parliament and a Marxist leader, who had visited Cuba for the eleventh World Festival of Youth and Students, held from 28 July to 5 August 1978 (it was attended by 18,500 people from 145 countries), and met Fidel Castro as part of a delegation from India. He had spent almost a week in the Caribbean nation along with M.A. Baby (then the student-wing leader of the Communist Party of India [Marxist] or the CPM), Prakash Karat (who later became the general secretary of the CPM), Mullappalli Ramachandran (Youth Congress leader), T.P. Dasan (former Mayor of Kozhikode district in northern Kerala) and the late Malayali film director Ramu Kariat.

My uncle recalled that thanks to Kariat, who had been to the country several times earlier, he and his friends could extensively explore Havana. They travelled and returned to India via the former Soviet Union and felt immense admiration for Cuba's people and leaders for their warmth and enthusiasm, but not so much with the stiff ways of the cadres of the Soviet communist party. 'We could sense the difference in the way people and the communist leadership in Cuba conducted things. They were more internationalist and loving than their counterparts in the Soviet Union who were plastic and combative,' he told me.

Rajan and other delegates were impressed with the security arrangements at the summit and were bemused when Castro appeared on the stage out of nowhere like Mandrake the Magician. Nobody could figure out how the Cuban leader had walked onto the stage unnoticed. Later, at a banquet thrown for delegates, Castro mingled with the crowds and Rajan was delighted to shake hands and exchange 'revolutionary' greetings with the legendary leader of Cuba, he recollected.

The first book by Che Guevara that I read in Malayalam was titled *Viplavathinte Ithihasam* (*Episodes of the Cuban Revolutionary War*), an autobiographical account of the Cuban Revolution to overthrow the dictatorship of Fulgencio Batista. The book talks about the time when Che met the Castro brothers Fidel and Raul in exile in Mexico after they were freed from jail following the 1953 uprising. A close reading of the work makes it abundantly clear that Raul and Che were the two hardcore Marxists of the group that led the Revolution. Besides the Castro brothers and Che, the group included Camilo Cienfuegos, Huber Matos, Juan Almeida Bosque, and others, some of whom were more amenable to a centrist rule than a pro-communist regime.

As a teen, I also had access to hundreds of articles on Cuba that Malayali Marxists, who had travelled to the

Caribbean country, had written or shared with us starting from 1991, in the tough years after the crumbling of the Soviet Union. This included works by those who hadn't been there, too, such as the late C. Bhaskaran, and those who had met Castro and shook hands with him, like M.A. Baby, who was then the leader of the CPM's youth movement. I also bought a handful of books and accessed non-fiction works by Indian and foreign authors translated into Malayalam from libraries. In the 1990s, one could also find copies of Guevara's *Motorcycle Diaries* published by New Left Books (Verso Books) and other works on Cuba in English bookstores in Thiruvananthapuram and other towns in Kerala. Although the Soviet Union is no more and communist rule is restricted to a few countries, books on Fidel, Cuba, and Che continue to sell like hot cakes in Kerala. Here is what a report in *The Hindu* in 2017 had to say about Che mania in Kerala:

> Before he was shot dead by Central Intelligence Agency (CIA)-trained troops in a remote village in Bolivia on 9 October 1967, Ernesto 'Che' Guevara, the revolutionary icon of the 20th century, had travelled by motorcycle through Latin American countries ravaged by colonialism, helped overthrow the Batista regime in Cuba, and held important positions in the Fidel Castro government, apart from authoring books on guerrilla warfare. Half a century after his death, the 'Comandante', as he was called by his followers, continues to evoke adulation in Kerala.[7]

Che Guevara had never been to Kerala, although he had spent two weeks in India in 1959—first in New Delhi where he met India's first prime minister, Jawaharlal Nehru, on 30 June, and then in Calcutta (now called Kolkata, the capital of West Bengal, where communist parties dominated as an electoral force for decades until their decline in the 2010s). While in Calcutta, Guevara stayed at the Indian Statistical Institute (ISI) in Kolkata for a few days. Shortly afterwards, in 1960, India opened its embassy in Havana. Although mainstream communists were not able to meet Guevara while he was in India, his visit to Kolkata is now regularly commemorated in West Bengal.

Guevara's daughter, Aleida Guevara, later visited many parts of India, including Delhi, Kerala and West Bengal, in a trip organized under the leadership of CPM leader M.A. Baby in 1997. As a young journalist then, I had the privilege of meeting her and witnessing how pleasantly surprised she was at the heroic welcome she received in several parts of Kerala. How did her father end up becoming an immortal hero in a place he had never been? That was the question she invariably raised. She was perplexed and thrilled to see herself appear in cartoons in Malayalam newspapers. During her visit decades later in early 2023, Aleida Guevara received an award instituted by the K.R. Gouri Amma Foundation.* She was felicitated for her efforts to rehabilitate differently abled children and provide debt relief to developing countries.

Cuba, in a sense, is also a metaphor in Kerala for so-called communist values—which are considered not very different from Gandhian values in the state. Most founding

---

* Gouri Amma was a legendary communist leader and female icon in Kerala.

communist leaders were members of Gandhi's Congress and
had internalized the values he had championed, including
self-reliance, simplicity and social harmony. Thus, they
brought to the communist movement in the state and
elsewhere a heavy dose of Gandhian idealism along with
their militant and unbending resolve to decimate dreaded
feudal practices that treated the working classes as fair
game. The communists in India competed with Congress
leaders to establish their credentials for simple living.

Which means ideological affinity isn't enough to win
respect. Which is why it is not difficult to fathom why
North Korea isn't seen as a respectable choice of role model
thanks to a dynasty running the show there. China is a
hostile neighbour to India and although communists are
proud of its meteoric growth as a military and economic
superpower and as a counterweight to the hegemony of
the United States, it is looked down upon by the romantic
communist lot for the 'pragmatic deviation' it has taken
after Mao.

On the other hand, Cuba is looked up to by Malayalis
in general as a country that has achieved miraculous strides
in education, medical research and healthcare. Incidentally,
the main character in a Malayalam movie titled *Arabikkatha*
(2007) is a dyed-in-the-wool communist named Cuba
Mukundan. The movie revolves around the travails of this
idealist. Although his character offers a certain comic relief
because of his anachronistic ways, it is incorrect to deduce
that it is a rebuke of Cuba, as some critics do.

The Cuban connection doesn't end there. I know a
Kerala-born magazine editor whose first name is Che; one
of my cousins has named his son Fidel; a Kerala government

officer bears the name Baby Castro; a character from another Malayalam movie *Pramani* (2010) is named Castro Vareeth; and V.S. Achuthanandan, one of Kerala's foremost Marxist leaders and a former chief minister, has earned the epithet, 'Fidel Castro of Kerala'. To say that Cuba has left an indelible imprint on the Kerala mindscape, especially among the leftists, is an understatement.

What's more, Che Guevara's name is pronounced differently in Kerala. It is uttered without a pause as 'cheguvera'. Instead of vara, the last syllable in his name, Malayalis say vera where 'e' is the 'e' of Mandela. A classic example of the 'Malayalification' of Che Guevara.

True, over time, alongside admirers, Cuban personalities have also attracted a set of detractors in Kerala who revel in trashing them—but there are no signs yet of the luminaries being ignored. Most critics paint Che as a sadist and others harp on the futility of the Cuban experiment. A few others point out that Kerala's Marxists had not been great admirers of the Cuban Revolution early on.

I had thought about the last accusation a lot and had dedicated a part of the obituary on Castro that I wrote on his death in 2016 to dwell on my doubts as a teenager over this argument.[8]

I wondered why there was not a single photograph of Che or Fidel at home (both maternal and paternal) while there were several huge ones of Marx, Engels, Lenin, A.K.G. (A.K. Gopalan), E.M.S. Namboodiripad, P. Sundarayya, Stalin and other local communist leaders of Kerala and Kannur. Even in the CPM 'party offices', there were none. When I could contain my curiosity no further, I asked a senior communist leader about it. 'We don't entirely agree with their party line' was the answer, which left me confused, disappointed and somewhat indignant.

Was their party line different? Why? Was our party line different from that of Antonio Gramsci, the Italian communist? My father, a popular CPM leader who died when he was just forty-one, had worshipped Gramsci. But I was glad to learn that though their 'party lines' were different, Kerala's Marxists, who take pride in coming to power through the democratic process, did bring out books on Guevera, Castro, Gramsci and so on through publishing houses they owned.

The reason why mainstream communists in India, those who had chosen the electoral path over armed struggle, didn't take great interest in the Cuban Revolution in its first two decades or so—until the beginning of the 1980s—was because they had to compete with the Naxalites, who had appeared to be a threat to them in the 1960s and the 1970s. Naxalite methods which relied on violence and Revolution had more in common with Castro's ascent to power as compared to the mainstream ballot-oriented Left. With the Naxalite movement in India declining by the late 1970s, the mainstream Left—especially the biggest constituent, the CPM—had no hesitation in lapping up heroic tales of the Cuban Revolution and its leading figures, especially Che and Fidel.

Funnily enough, Argentine icon Diego Maradona's triumph in the 1986 FIFA World Cup also embellished further the cult status of Che Guevara who was also Argentine, and Fidel Castro, who was destined to become the footballing icon's friend and saviour. The love and fascination for Maradona in the football-crazy state of Kerala knows no bounds. Later, Maradona endorsing Che with a tattoo on his right arm only helped create more buzz about the revolutionary icon. Maradona's medical treatment in Cuba, where he received rehabilitation therapies in 2000 for drug addiction and alcoholism, brought the Caribbean nation to the fore among football fans in Kerala once again. Maradona became synonymous with Cuba, too, besides, of course, Argentina, which, to date, remains the all-time favourite team among a majority of Malayalis, who had before the advent of Maradona cheered for Brazil.

Kerala's fondness for Cuba turned into tangible support after the Caribbean country lost its biggest communist ally. After the US imposed sanctions on Cuba—which began in 1962 and are the longest in modern history—it was the Soviet Union that provided Cuba with oil, food and machinery. The strong Soviet backing had meant annual subsidies worth up to $5 billion that helped Castro build reputable health and education systems. Between 1989—when cracks began to appear in the Soviet Union and aid tapered off—and 1991, the Cuban economy shrunk by 35 per cent.

During what is known in Cuba as the 'Special Period' (between 1991 and 2000) following the disintegration of the Soviet Union, scores of left-wing leaders from Kerala visited Cuba in large groups. Many of them had carried bags of rice and other grains. I had worked with volunteers in Kerala to collect donations for what was called the 'Cuban Relief Fund'. The situation in Cuba improved thanks to Venezuelan help towards the end of the 1990s, and after

Vladimir Putin came to power in Russia. US-led sanctions, of course, continue and are discussed later in the book, but these lines from an essay by Marquez titled 'Cubans and the Blockade' capture the gravity of the sanctions when they were first imposed in what was considered an exotic and permissive holiday destination of the American elite before the Revolution:

> That night, the first day of the blockade (3 February 1962), there were in Cuba some 482,550 cars, 343,300 refrigerators, 549,700 radios, 303,500 TV sets, 352,900 electric irons, 288,400 fans, 41,800 washing machines, 3,510,000 wrist watches, 63 locomotives and 12 merchant ships. All these, except the watches which were Swiss, were made in the United States. [9]

The books and documentaries I have read or watched on Cuba since I started working as a journalist in Delhi in the late 1990s have only rekindled my teenage passion for Cuba. Since 1959, the little nation has withstood the might of the American empire with its plots to engineer regime changes, assassination attempts on its top leaders, especially Fidel Castro, and the cruel sanctions to crush the spirit of the nation. Edwardo Galeano, the Latin American historian and football writer, once wrote about how rumours about the end of Castro had begun as early as the 1960s. In 1986, he wrote about one such 'prediction' in his mocking humour, 'Well-informed sources in Miami were announcing the imminent fall of Fidel Castro, it was only a matter of hours.'[10] The Special Period of the 1990s saw a raft of books, especially by journalists who had not been to

Cuba in years, who predicted Castro's collapse. As if to defy all his opponents, Castro took another twenty-odd years to die, hitting ninety before he passed on.

Here's what I wrote in an obit on Fidel Castro as a survivor against seemingly insurmountable odds:

After the 1959 revolution, he (Fidel Castro) gave the former Spanish colony and gambling destination famous for its rum, rumba and roulette a national identity; following the aborted Bay of Pigs war (April 1961)[*] and the Cuban missile crisis[†] in 1962 in which the US had to retreat from its earlier intention to attack Cuba in the face of a nuclear conflagration with the Soviet Union, he converted the former 'protectorate' of the US into a socialist showpiece. He also survived more than 600 assassination attempts using the most creative ways. In a mission named Operation Mongoose, the CIA planned to poison his cigar. They also tried to insert a kind of powder in his boots that would lead to the loss of his

---

[*] The Bay of Pigs attack of April 1961 was an aborted military invasion of Cuba at the Bahía de Cochinos (Bay of Pigs) planned by Central Intelligence Agency (CIA). Launched from Guatemala, it was led by Cuban exiles who landed on Cuban soil on 17 April and were defeated within two days by Cuban armed forces under the direct command of Castro.

[†] The Soviet Union placed nuclear missiles in Cuba pointing towards the US with the aim of protecting Cuba from any likely attack from the US or its proxies. As a result, in 1962, the two powerful military powers came to a standoff between 16 October and 28 October, bringing the world to the brink of a nuclear war. Moscow and Washington D.C. finally agreed to withdraw their missiles, from Cuba and Turkey, respectively, to resolve the dangerous crisis.

famed beard, and attempted to poison his food with the help of mafia groups. Fidel survived them all. He used the exodus from Cuba in the 1980s and the 1990s to get rid of political dissidents and criminals by emptying jails. He survived 10 American presidents and the boycott of the Roman Catholic Church until Pope John Paul II finally visited Havana in 1998. He survived his Cold War enemies as well as his allies. As declassified American documents reveal, he outlived and outdid powerful men and their plots to eliminate him for decades.[11]

Another reason for a Malayali to feel a special affinity for Fidel has to do with his love for drumsticks (moringa), which are perhaps consumed more in Kerala and other south Indian states than in any other part of India. After all, we cannot have our sambar without a generous dash of this ingredient. For 'Comandante' Castro, the drumstick was the denouement to a long search for a nutritious meal for the poor. Cuban scientist Concepción Campa Huergo helped him with this effort. She is quoted in a report saying that Castro showed great interest in developing this plant in Cuba, 'where tons of seeds arrived from India'.[12] The report added that moringa has been the focus of multiple studies, showing encouraging results in different diseases including anaemia, arterial hypertension and diabetes. 'We are in love with this plant, also called the tree of life, the light of hope,' said Campa Huergo. Cuba currently has three moringa factories that produce powdered dried leaves, with moringa seeds and oil available for purchase at pharmacies. Campa Huergo had travelled to Kerala to collect local varieties of drumstick seeds.

The titles she possesses are a confirmation of her stature in the country's scientific fraternity. Campa Huergo is an honorary doctor of the University of Havana and the Superior Institute of Medical Sciences of Villa Clara. She is also a senior researcher at the Ministry of Science, Technology and Environment. She explained to me in an interview that the biggest trigger for Fidel Castro to pursue the cultivation of drumsticks on a large scale was the Haiti earthquake of 2011, the year that country was also hit by a hurricane and a cholera epidemic. Castro always knew about the existence of the moringa plant and its nutritional and medicinal properties. Campa Huergo quotes the great Cuban leader as saying, 'All my life, I've been looking for a plant like this to reduce hunger and disease in the world, and I have finally found it.'

His logic was to cultivate the 'superfood' in all of Cuba, teach the Cuban population and other countries of the world to use it for human and animal consumption, and conduct research to study its medicinal properties to alleviate diseases and common health problems. She narrates what happened next: 'Fidel Castro dedicated the last five years of his life to this project. And to carry it out, he met with several Cuban scientists and sent them to various countries of the world to learn more about moringa, its cultivation and its uses. In their studies, they learnt that India was the country that had more experience in its production and use as food and for medicinal uses.'

She goes on, 'Cuban scientists visited various countries in Latin America, Europe, Africa and Asia from where different varieties of seeds were brought to Cuba, but it was really in India that the largest plantations of moringa were found and the possibility of buying all the tons of seeds that were needed to establish their cultivation throughout Cuba.'

It was Campa Huergo who travelled to India, including Kerala, but it was from Coimbatore in Tamil Nadu, Kerala's eastern neighbour, that the Cubans collected the PKM1 (Plain and Supergenius)[13] moringa varieties. Tons of moringa seeds were shipped from here to Cuba.

Campa Huergo tells me that, in Cuba today, the cultivation of moringa is spread across the island and the key objectives are to produce oil, animal fodder and for multiple uses in the pharmaceutical and food industries.

The senior scientist adds that Cuban experts have studied the benefits of moringa consumption 'in its functional food condition that not only benefits the nutritional status of the population, but also helps in disease prevention and control, including its effects on diabetes, anaemia, and arterial hypertension, among others'. They have set up a facility for investigating the benefits of moringa: the Centre for Research in Protein Plants and Bionatural Products, known by its acronym CIPB.

She further says, 'One of the key results from the study of the benefits of the moringa has been its use during pregnancy to combat anaemia, low baby weight at birth and other problems of motherhood, including improving the nutritional status of mothers.'

Cuba currently has three moringa factories—in the provinces of Havana, Sancti Spiritus and Pinar del Rio— for producing powdered dried leaves, moringa seeds and oil that are sold at pharmacies. A fourth factory is under construction in Santiago de Cuba.

'Much more remains to be done,' says Campa Huergo about Castro's dream.

For Malayalis with progressive political views, Cuba is somewhat like their own state, notwithstanding the latter's greater geopolitical significance and history of struggle against multiple empires. Ashok Alexander, founder-director of the public health nonprofit Antara Foundation, has this to say about the two geographies that he calls 'curious cousins':

> What do Kerala and Cuba have in common? To start with, they are both small places—Kerala has a population of only 33 million and Cuba is one-third of that. Both have a high female literacy rate, with Kerala at 97.9% and Cuba at 99%. Both have achieved a stage of zero population growth. And, if you believe it makes a difference (I don't), both have embraced a socialist-communist ideology for a long time. The most important similarity is that they are both winners in public health delivery, especially maternal and child health. Their health outcomes compare with those of the world's developed countries.[14]

So, when I flew for the first time into Havana's José Martí Airport from New Delhi via New York on a journalist visa in the summer of 2023, I was overwhelmed by the images of larger-than-life figures of the Cuban Revolution and powerful emotions, including a strange sense of familiarity with my destination and its people. My curious cousins, here I come!

Soul-Searching in Cuba

The sun is hot as hell, but the wind isn't. Which makes the weather sort of okay.

That is the first thing you notice when you sit back in what they call a *fotingo* or 'classic car' in Havana in the month of June. These vintage cars, relics of Cuba's pre-communist past, survive because of their ingenuity, so claim their proud owners without exception, as though it is the default statement to make. They are themselves very often the chauffeurs, too. This 'ingenuity' they are proud of is similar to what is termed as *jugaad* in India—the philosophy of being creative and making do with less. Chauffeur Alex, a strong black Cuban dressed like a cowboy, who takes me around Habana Vieja (Old Havana), Vedado and Miramar, the three main localities of the Cuban capital, tells me that most drivers (who are also invariably owners of these vehicles) are pretty good mechanics and know how to fix their cars if there is a problem. They don't have much choice in the face of uncertain supplies of parts for these mostly American cars due to hostile ties with the neighbouring superpower. 'I am a mechanical wizard, having driven this car for the past fifteen years and repaired it almost every day,' he says.

The Cubans too have a concept similar to jugaad—
resolver. In Spanish, the word means 'to solve'. But in this
island nation, the word (in which v is pronounced b) has
acquired a much deeper meaning, thanks to the sanctions
and the consequent shortage of goods. Making do with what
you have is the core of the 'resolber' philosophy, like jugaad.
Interestingly, a shooter game named Far Cry 6, developed
by Ubisoft, is inspired by this Cuban approach to life.[1]

The Oldsmobile convertible I am sitting in is neither
very comfortable nor convenient, but then I have no high
expectations. The car shudders around turns, but it also
makes you look like a mover and shaker on the roads
of Havana, except in Miramar, which houses upscale
residences and foreign missions. Elsewhere, there are
large queues of people waiting to board the *guagua* who
look at you, gravely curious, as you drive past in style in
your *fotingo**. These vintage cars make you look rich and
powerful, or so you think. Since you must pay $50 per hour
for this ride, you are entitled to this perception, all the more
so when you are the only occupant of the car besides the
person who drives you around. The chauffeur makes you
feel like royalty by opening the door for you. He has to,
because there is no way you can get out of this two-door
car other than by performing a high jump if he doesn't. The
door is in the front and you are seated at the back.

The fotingo are cars from Ford, Chevrolet, Cadillac, and
Chrysler. Then there are the old Russian ones—the Ladas,
Volgas and Geelys—besides the Russian Moskvitch 2141.
Some of the other brands include DeSotos, Plymouths

---

* A rental car, often a vintage vehicle

and Oldsmobiles. According to figures from 2014 (the last available), there are about 60,000 classic cars on the streets of Cuba, most of them in Havana.[2] All these cars, according to their owners, are precious heirlooms passed on from grandfathers to sons and now grandsons. They are painted well and made to look classy and are often parked in a row. Any photo you take of these cars in the foreground with the breathtaking Havana skyline behind is a postcard-worthy image, never mind that some of them are jalopies or what the Cubans call *cacharro*.

For inter-city transport, Cubans rely mostly on trains and jugaad transport—trucks. Tourists mostly travel in chartered buses that connect Havana to the rest of the cities and tourist spots like the UNESCO-listed Viñales and Pinar del Río. The large air-conditioned buses I saw were the Chinese-made Yutong buses from Zhengzhou Yutong Group Company. Empresa de Omnibus Nacionales (EON or National Bus Company), which falls under the ministry of transport, offers interprovincial bus transportation—all on Yutong buses.

The buses operated by EON for Cubans who pay in Cuban pesos (CUP) have a long waiting list, unlike those for tourists who pay in dollars. I was told that people have to book three months in advance to procure a confirmed ticket to avail of such transport services between provinces. Viazul, the bus service from EON for foreign tourists, plies between provinces, and the payment is done in dollars through credit cards, which means Cubans cannot use this. Transtur, a transport company of the ministry of tourism, provides transfer services within Havana. There are also hop-on-hop-off buses for city tours. Yutong is used for almost all these services and only the logo and the colour of the buses are different.

In Cuba, which faces fuel shortage and the impact of spiralling fuel prices, the various modes of travel also include *colectivos* or bicycle taxis; *camiones* or trucks. For short distances, there are coco-taxis, which are basically miniature versions of Indian auto-rickshaws and are in the shape of a coconut. During the Special Period, in the face of an acute transport crisis, the government had to put to use what are known as *camellos*, which are eighteen-wheel trucks converted into city buses. 'With black humour, Cubans call them "Saturday night movies" because of the adult language, sex and violence on board,' said a report in Reuters back in 2007.[3] Trucks-turned-buses are a recurring feature across most of the Third World. Flying is the easiest—albeit most expensive option—to travel from Havana to other cities down south including Baracoa, Cienfuegos, Guantánamo, Holguín, Santa Clara, Santiago de Cuba and Varadero and a few other destinations as well.

Alex takes me to the parking area next to Havana Cathedral, also known as Catedral de San Cristóbal, in the Plaza de la Catedral in Habana Vieja and then directs me to the church inside. 'I will wait for you,' he says. I realize that it has been a dehydrating drive, and the first thing I want to do is quench my thirst. By some divine intervention, I run into a man selling tender coconut water. He chops the coconut in the same fashion as they do in Kerala, with a *vettukathi* (felling knife or coconut cleaver). I drink it directly from the coconut shell without a straw and order another because it tastes quite like the ones we get in South India. The familiarity comforts me.

I walk slowly around the cathedral compound angling for a good view to take a photo, marvelling at how untouched and unaffected it looks by communism. For someone who had read Fidel Castro's conversation with Frei Betto on religion, I wasn't surprised that the motifs of the past as well as traditional and Christian rituals were allowed to coexist with communist ideology. If not earlier, at least since the dawn of this century, cultural and religious symbols of the country are gaining prominence.

Communist parties around the world have changed their stance on religious beliefs. In Kerala, not only are the Kerala Marxists more accommodative of 'believer's concerns' as opposed to total denigration of such sentiments, but they are also now using religious platforms to pull in votes. They do not want to be seen as anti-believers and frequently use symbols, insignias and figures important to multiple religions and sects in their campaigns and hoardings. This is indeed a big departure, and a sign of expediency. In China, the ruling communist party is looking to revive old traditions[4] in an apparent effort to check the effervescence of an organized religion, namely Christianity.[5]

Communist parties, in general, now want to project themselves as forces of resistance against divisive political outfits and global hegemons and not as ideologically rigid entities inimical to religious and ancient beliefs. In Cuba, too, the ruling party takes more pride in its patriotic and nationalist struggle against the United States rather than highlighting 'class war' or ideological confrontation. As Richard Gott, a historian and journalist familiar with Cuba and Latin America, points out, Cuba 'no longer justifies its existence on the attempts it once made to construct socialism'.[6]

In his 2005 work titled *Cuba: A New History*, Gott had predicted, 'When Castro dies, there will be little change in Cuba. While few people have been looking, the change has already taken place.'[*]

Well, it isn't easy to contest this statement because geopolitical compulsions seem to be dragging the country in a direction from where it has no choice but to adapt and face new economic challenges besides trying to meet the aspirations of its people. The need to change, therefore, has acquired political, economic and psychological dimensions.

I stand in the corner of the church watching the priest recite prayers in a building not far from a melancholic statue of Pope John Paul II, an avowed anti-communist for whom the end of the Soviet Union couldn't have come sooner. The dexterity of the government in sensing global

---

[*] Scholar Helen Yaffe disagrees with Gott on this point. She told me she had discussed the issue with Gott since, according to her, 'the end of his book missed key developments post-2000, including the Battle of Ideas, which reasserted the political commitment to socialism and the role of consciousness in that'. 'The Battle of Ideas' is a multi-faceted campaign launched by Fidel Castro in 1999 to reassert socialist values. Yaffe believes that 'he (Gott) was too pessimistic too soon'. Perhaps Gott amended his stance a bit after their discussion. In his blurb for Yaffe's book *We Are Cuba*, he wrote, 'Yaffe's book on the last thirty years of the Cuban Revolution explains why, in the absence of the two Castro brothers, it has not just survived but pioneered new forms of socialism suitable for the twenty-first century.'

undercurrents and suavely adapting to them is palpable. The credit for bringing in this change goes to the Castro brothers and the late Ricardo Alarcón (1937-2022), a fellow guerilla fighter and former minister. As Gott says:

> Many surprising weapons have been called into service to wage this battle (to influence public opinion and survive while being on their own, unsupported by any empire). Museums in the revamped sections of Old Havana ignore the achievements of the island's socialist era and sing praises of Spanish colonialism. Plantation culture and slavery, which only formally ended in 1886, are romanticised rather than excoriated. Former gangster hotels welcome foreign tourists with photographs of the good old days of rampant capitalism, when Argentinian tango stars, Mexican dancers, and Brazilian singers rubbed shoulders with the American mafia. Cuba has embraced 'heritage culture' with all the enthusiasm of the postmodernists in the West.

He adds that this culture of selective nationalist nostalgia is surely helping to fuel the country's ineluctable drive towards a capitalist future.

We don't know yet if all of Gott's arguments will come true in full measure since the communist party is still in power, presiding over the destiny of the people of this island nation while upholding Marxism-Leninism, a doctrine that emphasizes the overthrow of capitalism. But, as he said, the Cuban government's intention of showcasing history is ostensibly to erase the recent past filled with hardship and shortages. Surely, symbolism holds great significance in

Cuban politics. The rest of the world considered it a freak accident when two white doves appeared at Fidel Castro's first speech in January to Cuba after the Revolution. But to a large section of the country's citizens who hold Santería beliefs[*], predominantly those of African origin—essentially the Yoruba people brought in as slaves from West Africa— the two birds were a potent sign from the heavens since the dove represents Obatalá, a divine king who moulds humans from clay.[7]

Dr Ivor Miller, a cultural historian and author of a paper published in 2000 titled 'Religious Symbolism in Cuban Political Performance', notes that the dove incident is 'one in a long history of examples in which Caribbean leaders publicly use symbols from local religions'.[8] He concludes that many Cubans read the tableau of the two white doves, one perching on Castro's shoulder, and the other on the rostrum, as 'evidence of Castro's selection by supernatural forces'.

He writes that coded performances in the Caribbean political arena often have dual implications: 'One is geared to impress upon the international press and those with capital invested in the country that the speaker is popular and will maintain the status quo; another is geared to the local population by using icons from their religious practices.' Since many of these symbols often exist in religions that are less mainstream and almost underground, 'their use

---

[*] Santería, also known as Regla de Ocha, Regla Lucumí, or Lucumí, is an African diasporic religion that developed in Cuba during the late nineteenth century. It arose through a process of syncretism between the traditional Yoruba religion of West Africa, Roman Catholicism and Spiritism.

dramatically implies that the leader is privy to local secrets and esoteric power,' he notes.[9]

After a close examination of the commemorative practices related to the failed Moncada Barracks attack of 1953, scholars Anita Waters and Luci Fernandes wrote that 'an aura of religiosity is cultivated around the victims of Batista's backlash against the rebels'.[10] They argue that the attempt of the rebels, meaning those led by Castro and others who led the Revolution against Batista, was to 'reinforce the status of the Moncada generation as the canonical generation of Cuban history'.*

Even if there was a period of enforced atheism in Cuba in the early years of the Revolution, such as debarring anyone who openly professed a belief in God from being a communist party member, there are no signs of it anywhere today. What it has become de facto is a sort of tropical Marxism that accommodates multiple streams of thought and belief systems. In 1991, the Cuban Communist Party removed atheism as a prerequisite for membership. One year later, Cuba amended its constitution to deem itself a secular state rather than an atheist state. It is an altogether different matter that the Cuban government reacted harshly to the Varela Project, a referendum launched by Catholic dissident Oswaldo Paya in 1998, seeking freedom of expression, a free press, and free elections. Several members of the project, named after the Cuban priest Félix Varela (1788–1853) and which collected signatures of

---

* A simultaneous attack was carried out on the same day on the Carlos M. de Cespedes Barracks in Bayamo, the capital city of the Granma province.

more than 11,000 Cuban citizens, were jailed in 2003 for being paid agents of the US. The Castro government also denied during the period that Cuba had any prisoners of conscience. Paya died in a car crash in 2012.

In 2014, the then US President Barack Obama and Cuban leader Raul Castro thanked Pope Francis for helping broker 'a historic deal to begin normalising relations between the United States and Cuba, after 18 months of secret talks over prisoner releases brought a sudden end to decades of Cold War hostility'.[11] A year later, after meeting Pope Francis, Raul Castro, who was once a Jesuit schoolboy, told reporters that he was considering a return to the church and when they laughed, he said, 'I'm serious.'

This suggests that the communist party leaders in Cuba have become flexible enough to change with the times and allow for greater religious liberty, although the country still has a single-party rule in place to safeguard its resources and run all its affairs.

I walk back to the coconut seller and order one more drink. After paying him, I turn to walk back to the car when I run into an ageing lady, a clairvoyant. She calls herself Senora Habana, but her real name is Adelaida, and she is eighty-two years old, but she looks much younger. She sits in a chair on the veranda of a building outside the church, smoking a cigar. Her seat is colourful and next to it is a table with images and figurines and photographs of deities I do not recognize. Besides the cards and the statues, there are two photos of her—one depicts her as a glamorous young lady. Next to the table on the left is the chair for the customer, less colourful than hers. Behind her sits a middle-aged man who looks like he could be her son or a nephew. I exchange some pleasantries with them both. The man translates my English for her and her Spanish for me. The jaded fortune teller gestures at me to sit, and her translator asks me if I want to know my future. I ask them about the future of the Cuban Revolution. Her smile disappears when she hears the translation of my words, and she waves at me to scoot.

My tryst with Cuba's cultural past has just started. If you know how to ask the right questions, which I learnt the hard way with Adelaida, you end up listening to invigorating conversations—or lectures—from Cubans irrespective of their political views. Cubans, it comes to you like a shock, do not hide their opinions to please their rulers. Later that week, I will meet communist functionary and government official Felix Mejias Ruiz. You would expect him to wear a shirt emblazoned with the famous image of a sickle and hammer or a bust of Fidel Castro or Che. Instead, you have the colonial-time symbol of Havana, La Giraldilla, which is the statue of a Taino woman (the Tainos are the indigenous people of the Caribbean) carrying a pine tree trunk in one hand and the Calatrava cross in a flagpole in the other.

La Giraldilla, after all, is an emblem of love.

Alex takes me to two places of great importance to the Santería religion, which on first impression—from the nature of its people and its proximity to nature—appears like a subculture, but it isn't. The first place I visit in the city that is considered holy by Santería practitioners is 'Havana Forest' or 'El Bosque', which features a forest of sorts. The green zone is adjacent to the city but appears far because of a certain serenity associated with it. Benign old trees, a small bridge, and a stream bejewelled with rocks shimmering in the sun invite you to leave your worldly cares behind and take a breather.

I am unhappy to notice that many of the open areas are littered, much like tourist spots in India. But standing there and watching the stream ripple against a backdrop of dark green trees with roots that resemble the varicose veins of an old person, I cannot help but feel a connectedness with nature. The stream is used for religious rituals including the sacrifice of chickens, I am told.

While I am there, I observe what looks like a fashion shoot in progress by the bank of the stream. A small team of four busy themselves around a tall black model in a sunset yellow gown and diamond tiara. An older, lanky white man in a plain T-shirt and cargo pants does her makeup while she balances herself on the rocks. Another old man with a red cap and red checked shirt fiddles with camera equipment and an older blonde woman stands by holding a bunch of clothes in her arms. I look at the landscape behind the model. I am sure the photographs would be worth the effort.

Alex then takes me to the Callejon de Hamel alleyway community art project, which prominently showcases open-air paintings and sculptures linked to Afro-Cuban culture. It was launched in the 1990s by artist Salvador Gonzalez Escalona and is now the most famous back alley in the city. The alley has been converted into a space for art and consistently promotes live music, Santería religion and African folklore. Travel books describe it as a 'sub-neighbourhood' of Centro Habana (Central Havana) called Cayo Hueso, which still resembles Belgian-born French film director Agnès Varda's pictures of post-revolutionary

Cuba that were used in her 1963 film *Salut les Cubains*. Cayo Hueso also finds mention in legendary Afro-Cuban filmmaker Sara Gómez's masterpiece, *De Cierta Manera* (One Way or Another). The film was released in 1977, three years after her tragic death at the age of thirty-one in 1974 from an asthma attack. The subcultural hues of the Santería religion are starkly visible in several parts of the country— clearly why the writer Pico Iyer made his character in *Cuba and The Night* state that, at times, the whole island felt like an 'African village dancing to Spanish guitars'.

According to a February 2021 report by the United States Commission on International Religious Freedom, 'Roughly 70 per cent of Cubans observe one or more Santería or other religious practices based in an African tradition. Elements of Santería and its African roots permeate Cuban culture, including by influencing Cuban art, food, music, and dance.'[12] It notes that Santería's syncretism traces its origin to the religious practices of the Yoruba people, who were brought centuries ago as slaves to Cuba from the Congo Basin and West Africa. The Santería religion was initially developed in secret and incorporates elements of Catholicism, which was the only religion permitted on the island by Cuba's Spanish colonial masters starting from the late fifteenth century. And so, Santería's religious practices were 'intermingled' with Catholicism.

Santería practitioners make physical offerings to deities, known as *orishas*, who typically have a Catholic counterpart. Having been a secret religion, Santería (which translates to 'the way of the saints') continues to operate through private homes and as informal societies—it has no centralized leadership.

That evening, dressed in khaki pants and a loose white shirt, Alex, a proud believer in the Santería religion, steps on the gas, raises the stereo volume, and shakes his head cockishly—as though his favourite football team just scored a surprise equalizer—to the heavenly beat of that dazzling song by Cuban trumpet player and songwriter Alexander Abreu Manresa, *Me Dicen Cuba* (They Call Me Cuba). We are on Quinta Avenue (Fifth Avenue).

I decide to go back to the hotel and look up the lyrics.

Aspiration Nation

In recent years, the population of Cuba has hit a downward curve. Its fertility rate fell from 4.5 in 1963, just after the Revolution, to 1.5 in 2020. Its total population—which hit a peak of 11.3 million in 2016—is estimated to be only as strong as 10 million even in 2050. Usually, a decline in the birth rate is linked to higher levels of development and women's education and emancipation. But in Cuba, there's another factor—outmigration.

The youth are leaving. Most likely, the Cuban population has already touched 10 million and there are claims that it has slid much further due to an exodus to the West over the past two years.

Basically, the youth don't want to shoulder the struggle that their parents' generation had undertaken in the name of the Revolution. They are not as invested in fighting off the globally condemned US embargo.

As the young waitress in my hotel in Vedado said, all that they want is freedom from perpetual economic uncertainties and the freedom to choose from a decent set of options, perhaps those that only a capitalist society can provide. They agree that they are beneficiaries of the country's free education and healthcare system. The scores of young men and women I spoke to—in bars and universities and workplaces—also concede that US sanctions on Cuba are a heinous crime against humanity as a whole. They know that multiple Popes and international organisations have either voiced their opposition or voted against these unilateral sanctions by the Americans. They are aware of geopolitics and can talk to you about the Elián González controversy of 1999–2000 for hours, from both the viewpoints of the Cuban–American community and Cuban politicians back home.* They know that the UN General Assembly has since 1992 been passing resolutions against the American violation of the Charter of the United Nations and of international law over these sanctions. They are also aware that Israel is the only other country that consistently joins the US in voting against the resolution.

Yet, their contention is this: they want nothing to hamper ease of living. They want to live and travel the way the middle classes in advanced and emerging nations do.

If the youth are the future, this is certainly a socio-political trend that cannot be ignored or swept under the carpet. Noted American behavioural economist Dan Ariely says there are marked differences between Cuba's younger generation and their parents', suggesting that the challenges

---

* González survived a boat wreck aged five while his mother and her boyfriend drowned as the trio, along with many others, tried to emigrate to the US. The coast guard saved González three miles from the Florida coast and American authorities handed him over to a relative in Little Havana, Miami, setting off a legal and diplomatic tussle between the US and Cuba because the boy's father in Cuba sought his custody. Finally, the son was united with the father and is now an engineer and a Cuban politician.

before the government, be it in Cuba or elsewhere, are huge. 'So many things could be different. Could be that they don't have the initial experience that the parents' generation had. It could also be the impact of social media. It could also be that Covid-19 has had a more tremendous impact in a far deeper way than we are recognizing today and in a different and more devastating way. How do we raise a generation of people who are more excited and more united and more connected is the question here. Social resilience is low and social connections are low. Those are the things to try and build,' he tells me.

Rebecca (name changed), a woman in her late twenties who works in the hospitality sector in Havana, says that those who receive remittances from their folks from overseas are much better off than others. She doesn't have that privilege, she tells me, adding that she is a trained psychologist but has to work in a hotel because that is the more viable option. 'My husband and I both work and my in-laws earn pensions, but we still skip one special item for lunch or dinner. For instance, if we cook eggs for lunch, we won't cook chicken for the same meal. We often must make such sacrifices to make ends meet.' She further says that anxieties about the future are palpable in all families.

The social resilience that Ariely talks about is not an attractive proposition for the youth. They are tuned into the changing lifestyles and cultural trends of their peers in other countries through social media—Facebook and Instagram are ubiquitous on mobile phones, and no politician can afford to be absent from Twitter, now called X. Even if the social-media accounts the youth follow represent only a small class out of the whole, the segment of youth connected online may be quite large when you include countries with a sizeable population such as India or China, both of which are estimated to have crossed 1.4 billion people each.

India's per capita GDP is roughly a quarter of Cuba's—about $2250 in India versus $9500 in Cuba—but many of India's middle classes have high disposable incomes that make their lives easy and worth living. In sharp contrast, in Cuba, the aspirations of even the highly educated Cubans are constrained by low pay. The difference in financial freedom then becomes glaring.

Again, there is a caveat: very few Cubans pay rent, most of them stay in their own homes, and education and healthcare are free. Plus, the government has subsidies for many other services, including food supplies, beverages, sports activities and entertainment. This means these low incomes are not to be compared with those in countries where people suffer from extreme poverty and are unsupported by their governments. The situation in Cuba is nowhere near there.

But what is disconcerting is that there is a huge disparity in the incomes of highly skilled people employed in the government, the biggest employer, and those who work in the tourism sector, who earn far more. This has forced several highly skilled employees of the government to quit and work in hospitality and tourism sectors, often taking up positions far below their qualifications. Many other skilled citizens, especially the younger lot, prefer to leave the country and struggle to make it big elsewhere.

Sample this: on a good day, a vintage car chauffeur in Cuba earns much more money than a qualified doctor earns in a month. So do those who run casa particulares, or private bread and breakfast homestays for tourists. Taxi drivers, the yellow cabbies, on the other hand, work for a government-run agency and must share their proceeds with the agency apart from taking responsibility for the repair work of the car.

When I was in Cuba in the summer of 2023, 1 US dollar or 1 euro was considered equivalent to 120 CUP (they treat euros and US dollars the same). The average wage in Cuba was 3830 CUP per month (INR 2640) in 2021, up from 1194 CUP per month (INR 823) in 2020, according to the National Office of Statistics, Republic of Cuba.[1] The first time I hired Alex, he charged me $200 (or 24,000 CUP or 16,500) for a full day's service—he brought his rates down a few notches once he got to know me better. In contrast, a general practitioner (GP) in Cuba earns around 5000 CUP (INR 3450) a month and a specialist doctor around 7000 CUP (INR 4830) per month, as I gathered based on my discussions with public health officials. Even the highest-earning engineers don't earn much more. Pensions for the retired are much lower, as low as 2000 CUP (about $16 or INR 1380) a month. Some retirees told me they receive around 1500 CUP (INR 1035). Understandably, these amounts are considered low by young graduates, which is why they relocate abroad for better prospects.

Expectedly, the ballooning aspirations of well-educated Cuban youth connected through the internet with peers around the world have led to frustration and a collective sense of #FOMO—fear of missing out. It has also led to a brain drain with young people flocking abroad with the hope of building better lives for themselves. Protests erupted in the country on 11 July 2021, shortly after the Covid-19 lockdown was lifted, as people hit the streets criticizing the government for the hardship and shortages of goods and services they had to face. The pandemic had displaced people from regular jobs and led to scarcity of food and medicines. The government, on its part, blamed the US for financing counter-revolutionaries and for taking advantage of the economic hardship caused by the US trade embargo, which had been tightened during the lockdown. (The US under Barack Obama had promised to lift sanctions, but Donald Trump went back on those promises in 2017.) Following the protests, Reuters quoted Cuban authorities as saying that the trouble was an outcome of the US's 'economic asphyxiation' of Cuba and its meddling in the affairs of the archipelago.

The 2021 protests led to structural changes and since then, Cubans have been allowed to incorporate small and medium-sized businesses which can employ up to 100 people. More than 8000 have already been registered—a significant number in a small population.

Another protest broke out three years later, on 17 March 2024, primarily in Santiago de Cuba, the country's second largest city, once again in the face of food shortages and power outages. Clearly, there was fatigue among people amid economic hardship. This time, too, the government of the Caribbean nation accused the US of interfering in their internal affairs and conveyed their formal disapproval to the US Chargé d'Affaires Benjamin Ziff, who was summoned to the Ministry of Foreign Affairs. A statement by the ministry followed, which stated, 'At the meeting, attention was also drawn to the direct responsibility of the US government for the difficult economic situation Cuba is going through at this time and, specifically, for the shortages and difficulties faced by the population on a daily basis, with the depression and insufficiency of supplies and essential services, under the weight and impact of the economic blockade designed to destroy the economic capacity of the country.' It added, 'The destabilising plan and its execution are evident for all to see. It rests on the reinforcement of a ruthless economic war to cause and burst the natural irritation of the population. It is financed every year with tens of millions of dollars from the US federal budget. It has a powerful technological infrastructure to operate digital networks from US territory and for aggressive purposes.'

People in Cuba I spoke to, however, state that the government, too, must take responsibility for omissions—which include the theft of tons of chicken from warehouses and the sloppy way food items are stored in cold-storage facilities. 'They are not taking proper care of the very little resources we have,' said one of them, a self-confessed 'radical', emphasizing that people were merely demanding basic needs and that the crackdown was unwarranted.

The doctors I met argued that they were not driven by any profit motive but by a sense of mission and patriotism. Many of them have worked in overseas destinations, mostly those hit by epidemics or natural or manmade calamities. They say they want just enough money to live decently, and the state provides them the perks, including housing and rations. The economists I met still speak of the spirit of the Revolution and the pledge to build a model society. But the younger generation isn't overly excited about it. 'We have heard it for long, but nothing has changed,' a young man

I met at the Havana University told me. The wage disparity became more conspicuous after 2021 with the presence of new small businesses, triggering an exodus of qualified young people.

One morning, while walking to the University of Havana from the Nacional de Cuba Hotel, a tall, skinny fellow approached me on the street, stating that the home on the second floor on our right side was his and that anything was possible in this country. 'Call me Fernando. I am your friend,' he announced and then asked my name and where I was going. He had some difficulty pronouncing it right and took it upon himself to accompany me to the university and walked along with me. He began to behave like a guide of sorts, describing to me the buildings on the way until I told him I wished to go alone and didn't need company. 'I am free. No problem,' he said, and we continued our march towards the university, two tall brown men with curly hair, walking in rhythmic cadence. I was reminded of my Sainik School days in Kerala when we matched our steps with our fellow students even during leisurely walks.

Fernando and I were both in jeans and sneakers, purchased in opposite corners of the globe. Somewhere along the way, he asked me for 1000 CUP (which is approximately INR 690), pleading, 'My baby hasn't eaten anything since morning, and I have to buy him something. My baby is waiting for me.' On the way, we saw a bedraggled middle-aged man begging motorists for cash at the traffic signal. 'No shame. Look, what he is doing!!' Fernando complained. This made me laugh. I looked at him curiously. 'I will give you 500 pesos. But you must go back,' I told him.

Fernando saw it as a humiliation. 'You give me 500 pesos after we reach the university,' he said. He is not *sanaco*[*], he asserted. 'Not a fool,' he translated. He continued to play the guide until we reached the steps of the university that had once been a hub of revolutionary activities in the years leading to the Moncada Barracks attack and finally the Revolution of 1959.

'Goodbye, friend. Call me. This is my number,' Fernando said, asking me to save his number. 'You have a local number?' he asked as an afterthought.

'Yes,' I responded.

'Tell me the number,' he paused, and then said, 'No. Call me if you want to. Save my number.'

I saved his number on my phone.

'My friend, anything is possible here, anything. Please call me,' he said again.

I watched him walk away like a pugilist. And it struck me that even though he was a stranger, he didn't make me feel uncomfortable or uneasy in any way. Walking with him was like walking with a friend I had known for long. I wondered why he decided against taking my local phone number.

What came to mind were lines from the song 'People Are Strange' by The Doors, immortalized by Jim Morrison in his unsurpassable baritone: *People are strange, when you're a stranger.*

I stood for a minute in the sun, admiring a bronze statue titled 'Alma Mater' made in 1919 by sculptor Mario Korbel. Then I walked up the steps of the university and

---

[*] A commonly used adjective in Cuba for a foolish person

past a security guard who looked at me but said nothing. Inside, I found students seated on benches preoccupied with their books and discussions. I kept walking until I found a group of five or six, mostly girls, who seemed to be in a joyful mood. They were seated not far from the bust of Rubén Martínez, a writer and revolutionary leader who died prematurely at the age of thirty-five from tuberculosis.

The students were waiting for more people to join them for a play practice. I hung around for a chat, their animated discussions revving me up. They were a heterogeneous group—some studying journalism, others foreign languages or economics. A few were still in their late teens, others a bit older. Then a new girl came running, apologizing for being late. She started hugging everyone one by one, including me. I am unaccustomed to hugging women in India—my Punjabi wife and her cousins poke fun at me for my Malayali reserve when it comes to hugs—but the Cuban student's friendliness and warmth overrode any awkwardness I felt.

I told another student next to me, 'Your friend thinks I'm one of you.'

'It's okay,' she smiled.

She told me her name was Jessica and that she was a student of journalism and communication at the university. 'There are fewer opportunities here than outside the country for journalism. Most are government-run and so I would like to travel and work once I complete my course,' she shared. Her family was one of the first to sign up for the private-sector licence, she said. Dressed in a fitted black halter-neck dress with a delicate gold chain around her neck, she appeared to be from a relatively well-off background. All her friends did too.

She said she was more interested in independent journalism, which wasn't robust in her country. 'We have problems, but then we have more problems because of the sanctions. One cannot analyse Cuba accurately without factoring in how it has been tormented through decades of boycotts. We have hardships but they are not something that cannot be solved. Cuba will change if isolationism by the US is stopped,' she stated.

Then she added, 'Of course, the government can allow for protests to happen because after all, there are protests in all countries and there is no need to stop people from protesting and venting their frustration. If TV channels show that people are protesting in Cuba, there is nothing unnatural about it. Such events take place all over the world.'

We are changing and we will change faster, that is my hope, she summed up as her friends gestured to her to join the practice.

I was about to invite her and all her friends to an evening drink, but I held back, unsure if they may be officially underage for drinking. 'Bye! Bye!' she hugged me and darted away. Her words echoed what Richard Gott had prophesied long ago: that change has been happening in Cuba without most people noticing it.

I sent my wife in Delhi a selfie I took with the young students, their faces lit up with big grins. 'Quite a smart, diverse lot,' she messaged back. 'Don't I look like a student too in this picture?' I asked, fishing for compliments. 'Maybe their dad,' she teased.

Around noon the next day, I decided to visit El Floridita, a historical fish restaurant. I was with a new chauffeur, and he asked for 1900 CUP (around $15 or INR 1260) for the short ride to the restaurant–bar from my hotel. He said he could drop me back, too, and I just had to call him on his cellphone once I was done. We exchanged numbers and I gave him a missed call from my local Cuba number.

The local telecom services company ETECSA offers excellent services including high-speed internet. It was a major source of solace for me because I could work remotely, and it busted the myth that the internet in Cuba was slow or non-existent. But there is a problem. Cuban students are unable to access Coursera or other online courses due to their location. They have to log in through a virtual private network (VPN) to do that. This is another ugly side of the embargo. I couldn't log on to my crypto exchanges, including my Pi Network app—a cryptocurrency with the widest reach, spanning across 230 regions worldwide—to continue mining. Even for entities like Pi Network, which promises the democratization of blockchain technology and lowering entry barriers for the common man, Cuba remains an outcast.

El Floridita was a revelation. Maybe that is the feeling everyone gets on their first visit here. It first opened in 1817. The crowd is cosmopolitan and affluent, in sharp contrast with the local population outside. I found a spot from where I could watch the bar and the band that stood playing next to a statue of Papa Hemingway, as he is called in this part of the world. The American writer patronized this restaurant more than half a century ago, his favourite drink being their legendary daiquiri, introduced in the early 1930s.

I ordered the Papa Hemingway Daiquiri, a cocktail of Havana Club rum, grapefruit juice and maraschino (a liqueur from Marasca cherries). I ordered two shots up front, sensing that the crowd was swelling and that the waiters would not be available later, and I was right. When I asked for a third shot, it took them more than twenty minutes to serve it. A shot was priced at 750 CUP (around INR 520). I then told the waiter I wanted to order Hemingway's favourite dish. He went around asking his colleagues what Hemingway's favourite food item was and came back saying nobody knew the answer. Hunger and rum combined to make me more impatient by the minute while the waiter continued his research with other, more senior employees. Overhearing all the talk, a prosperous-looking Mexican man next to me offered to Google the answer. He was not successful. Another lady seated a row away, who was listening to all the commotion, joked, 'Maybe Papa Hemingway ate nothing. He only drank.' She repeated the same thing in Spanish for her friends at her table.

I gave up and placed an order for a Sandwich de Serrano (containing ham and serrano pepper). It arrived quickly and made for a delicious lunch.

When the music stopped for a while, a couple came over smiling to my table and struck up a conversation. When I said I was a journalist from India, they said they thought I was from Dubai. The prosperous middle-aged couple said they wanted to travel to India but were worried about the global image that Delhi has: of being unsafe for women and tourists. They had been to South Africa, and we swapped stories of Gandhi Square and Robben Island. Delhi is any day safer than Johannesburg, I said, and assured them that they now have a new friend there. Their faces glowed and they expressed their gratitude in advance.

I asked them which country they were from. They said they were Cubans. I asked, 'From Miami?' The husband nodded, 'We spend some months here and then go back to Miami.' He was wearing an expensive chain around his neck like Al Pacino in *Scarface*. We have a home and all amenities here too, they added. The husband went on to brag about having eaten crocodile meat the previous night. 'Do you want to try rhombifer meat?'*

I didn't answer, but my guess was right. Tourists don't fly down here with Mercedes saloons and brand-new American cars. More luxury cars on the road meant more non-resident Cubans were here, and possibly, the presence and power of Cuban Americans in Cuba was growing.

When I left after another shot of Papa Hemingway, the band was rocking away and young women and men on holiday were jiving and laughing their hearts out while the older ones watched.

Once outside, I called the driver who was already there. The sun was bright, and I felt it on my face. I calculated the dollars I had paid and realized that, at El Floridita, they used a different calculation for currency conversion, favouring the dollar: One dollar was treated as equivalent to 150 CUP as opposed to 120 CUP elsewhere.

But then, the dollar currency rate is a fluid organism in Cuba. When I had sought help earlier through an embassy, in exchange for $100, they paid me 19,000 CUP, which meant $1 was worth 190 CUP. Some others say a dollar can fetch you 250 to 310 CUP in informal markets. Every day brings new calculations.

---

* A small species of crocodile endemic to Cuba

'I should have invited you to join me in El Floridita,' I told the driver out of a sense of guilt and perhaps also because I was slightly tipsy.

'No. I have to drive,' he said and thanked me.

As he drove me along the Malecon where waves crashed merrily on the seawall, we spoke about Cuban Americans from Miami—the hotbed of anti-Castro sentiment and pro-sanction lobbying—returning to Cuba. He said, 'These people come and go more frequently (than before).'

'Is it a good trend? Will they help in lifting the sanctions and revitalize the economy?'

My driver remained silent. My question turned into a metaphorical thought, befitting the end of a conversation.

The Sin of Sanctions

Cubans never use the term 'sanctions'. For them, it is *el bloqueo*—'blockade'. Diasporic Cubans aren't all wishing for the Caribbean nation to disappear from the face of the earth or even longing for regime change, argues Ambassador Cabañas, a legendary figure in Cuban diplomacy. When he was named Cuba's ambassador to the US in September 2015, Dr José Ramón Cabañas Rodríguez became the first one to occupy a post that had lain vacant for more than half a century—fifty-four years precisely. He had already been posted in the US as the chief of the Cuban Interests Section in Washington D.C. since 30 October 2012, when he was promoted to this position.[1] His stint as ambassador lasted until 21 December 2020. Yet, it saw a massive shift in relations between the two countries and the visit in 2016 of President Barack Obama to Cuba, the first such event since 1928.

Indeed, the two neighbours had strained relations so intense that they not only led the world to the brink of a nuclear war in 1962 but had also earlier resulted in a failed US-sponsored invasion of Cuba in 1961 to engineer a regime change, and numerous assassination attempts over the decades on Cuban leaders, especially Fidel Castro. The US-sponsored and financed Bay of Pigs invasion of Cuba, led by Cuban exiles (called the 2506 Brigade), turned out to be a humiliating defeat for the American establishment that had planned this disastrous misadventure. Castro's forces captured over 1,100 men, who were later released in exchange for $53 million worth of food and medicine between December 1962 and July 1965. Cuban exiles were put into action by the Americans repeatedly over the next decades to overthrow the Fidel Castro-led communist government in Cuba, but to no avail.

Obama reversed the decades-long policy—although he never lifted the sanctions or stopped the funding for 'democracy-promotion' or regime-change programmes and only resumed diplomatic ties with the promise of getting rid of them—of ten previous US presidents for whom isolating Cuba was a pillar of their foreign policy. The Obama push started with a trip to Havana by John Kerry in July 2014, the first US secretary of state to visit the country in seventy years. Obama's logic was that American foreign policy had failed to promote democracy or improve the lives of people in Cuba. 'It hasn't worked for fifty years. It shuts America out of Cuba's future, and it only makes life worse for the Cuban people,' Obama said then, but continued to assert that it was against media control by the communist party and the silencing of dissidents. For its part, Cuba maintained that it had to take strong actions because most dissidents, its officials said, were sponsored by the US to destabilize the country.

Barack Obama and Raul Castro initiated talks in 2014, and the two nations restored diplomatic ties in 2015.

Benjamin J. Rhodes, former deputy national security advisor for strategic communications and speechwriting under Obama, also played a crucial role in the parleys along with several others. In 2017, however, the newly elected US President Donald Trump stalled Obama's historic rapprochement with Cuba and cancelled what he described as a 'one-sided' deal by Obama with Cuba. He did it to please one constituency, the Cuban exiles, who voted in his favour. But Trump did so in phases, allowing for normalization of relations in his first two years and then backtracking on the progress later.

Ambassador Cabañas tells me in a meeting I had with him in the afternoon of 19 June 2023 at his office in the Research Centre for International Policy (CIPI) in Havana that the myth of the Cuban-American being rabidly anti-Cuba goes with a template that is popularized by those who benefit from such a narrative. So is the impression, he argues, that all Americans are supportive of the sanctions on Cuba. In fact, a Pew study published in December 2016 suggested that as much as three out of four Americans were in favour of *ending* the long-standing US trade embargo against Cuba.[2]

Cabañas points out an interesting phenomenon to buttress his arguments. In Republican-majority Florida, in which Miami falls, abortion is outlawed, and therefore, if a woman of Cuban descent (whoever is born in Cuba is considered a citizen of the country by the government in Havana) needs an abortion, all she has to do is fly down 90 miles south to Havana and get an abortion for free—thanks to the free medical care in the country—and then fly back. The process is smooth, and you have the best of both worlds.

In Havana, Escuela Latinoamericana de Medicina (ELAM), or the Latin American School of Medicine, admits students from as many as 110 countries, mainly from Latin America, Africa, Asia and the United States. According to officials, tuition, room and board are free and the students are offered a small stipend. These students often spread the word among Cuban-American women looking for termination of unwanted pregnancies.

Economic crises and migration have a strange relationship. Cabañas, who speaks with the candour of a serious academic and the skill of a diplomat, notes that at the end of 2018, illegal migration from Cuba to the US touched its lowest levels—meaning zero in those months. Why and how? Because there was hope that the normalization of relations would eliminate the hardships of life that Cuban people were facing because of the sanctions. 'When they don't squeeze us economically, we don't have migration,' he says, adding that, without Cuba specifically asking for it, the US also implemented a comprehensive set of measures at the time: more regular flights to Cuba and back, and a five-year visa (basically for families), which eased the pressure to emigrate.

Under Obama, Cuba and the US signed twenty-two memoranda of understanding (MoUs) and set in motion a process for rapprochement. These agreements covered a variety of topics, including civil aviation, agriculture, search and rescue, fighting oil spills in the Caribbean Sea, and law enforcement, which incorporated different subjects from cyber-attacks to terrorism. In the initial years, President Donald Trump let the status quo continue, which is why Cabañas divides the Trump administration into two phases: 2017 to 2019 and from 2019 to 2021.

'The first two years were a period in which no dramatic changes were introduced,' the seasoned career diplomat says, adding that 2018 and 2019 saw the largest amount of travel on both sides, from the US to Cuba and Cuba to the US.[*] According to World Tourism Organization figures, tourism inflow to Cuba rose steadily from 2.98 million tourists in 2014 to 4.71 million in 2018.[3] Numbers crashed to a little over a million in 2020, the year of the pandemic.

But the sector has, according to stats disclosed by Cuban tourism authorities, improved since 2022.[4] In 2023, as of 1 August, the country's Tourism Ministry (MINTUR) said it received more than 1.2 million tourists amid a steady increase in Russian tourist arrivals. By the end of 2023, this figure was 2.4 million.[5]

In 2018, notwithstanding his public posturing, the Trump administration provided a licence for a joint venture (JV) between New York-based Roswell Park Cancer Institute and Cuba's Center for Molecular Immunology, which falls under the umbrella organisation of BioCubaFarma, the Cuban organization of Biotechnology and Pharmaceutical Industries, which has scores of companies in its fold. Thanks to the JV, called The Innovative Immunotherapy Alliance SA, the American partner intended to bring to the US a Cuban lung cancer drug named CimaVax-EGF. Roswell Park said it had raised $4 million in donations to fund the clinical trials of the CimaVax EGF drug.[6]

---

[*] With the probable exception of when, in November 2017, the US withdrew most of its embassy staff and shut the consulate, forcing Cubans to travel to third countries to apply for visas

Again, although President Donald Trump had partially unravelled the historic US-Cuba détente[7], it was under his watch that Cuba tied up with health authorities for cooperation in the city of Chicago and organized in the US, between 8 and 20 May 2018, the biggest-ever Cuban cultural festival in which 400 Cuban artists took part, Cabañas recalled.[8]

By early 2019, events in Venezuela, which has the world's largest oil reserves, plunged it into a political and economic crisis, and Trump, who accused Havana of supporting Nicolás Maduro in the South American country, imposed more sanctions on Cuba and withdrew Obama's Cuba policy. The American policy was an act of punishment without giving the Cubans a chance to be heard. Cabañas remembers an American official telling him, 'Venezuela will fall soon, and you will fall in a few months.'

'That is how these people speak, but then their forecasts didn't come true,' he told me. Even so, Cuba was dragged into an economic crisis, and with the coming of the Covid-19 pandemic in 2020, 'it was like we had two embargoes on us, one by the Americans and the other by the pandemic,' he explained.

Soon, everything changed in the name of votes, stated Cabañas.

It isn't difficult to see why. Florida was a swing state once, and it was always said that a Democrat could win the US Presidential polls even without winning in Florida, but a Republican could not do the same. Florida is now home to a brand of politics that is anti-Cuba, but it wasn't like this in more than two decades after the Revolution. It took systematic funding by Republicans to create an anti-Cuba bloc among Cuban Americans. This was no organic political evolution, but part of a project worth millions of dollars to ensure that Florida went with the Republicans.

This political ploy was masterminded by Ronald Reagan, who came to power in 1981 by replacing Jimmy Carter. Even before he became president, Reagan, in 1980, had made a strong statement about Cuba as regards the potential evacuation of Cubans who did not wish to live in the archipelago. It was when he was at the helm as President that the US Government created Radio Martí to air anti-communist propaganda, targeting a regime change in that country. It was done at the request of Florida-based Cuban-American businessman Jorge Mas Canosa. *The Washington Post* reported on 25 March 1984 about the political churning among Cubans in Florida:

> In this climate of intense anti-communism, Reagan's policies and rhetoric have produced a groundswell of support for the GOP (Republican Party). A political realignment of the Cuban community is pushing Florida, a key swing state in presidential and senatorial elections, toward the Republican column.

The report also carried stereotypical perceptions lapped up for convenient reasons by the Cuban community in the US: that they were political dissidents who had great prosperity back home in Cuba before Castro came in.

Wen Wang writes in a 2022 paper titled 'Reagan and Cuba: an analysis of U.S. foreign policy in the 1980s':

> In the mid-1970s, President Jimmy Carter made several conciliatory gestures almost immediately after

his inauguration, conveying the message that efforts to improve relations with Cuba would be one of the administration's top priorities. Compared to the 1970s, the economic embargo was significantly stricter in the Reagan years. In July 1986, the Reagan administration tightened the embargo again to force Cuba back to the negotiation table over radio broadcasts and the renewal of the immigration accord.[9]

Wang says that Reagan's antagonistic attitude and Castro's unwillingness to play a helpful role in getting Reagan re-elected, as the American leader had hoped, delayed the negotiations. For most of Reagan's time in power, US-Cuban relations fell to new lows compared with the previous two presidencies.

Cabañas and I met at his office at the Research Centre for International Policy (CIPI) where he is currently the director. The institute falls under the Cuban Ministry of Foreign Affairs. I was late from a previous meeting and so I was glad that he too was late. He walked in apologizing profusely for being late, although his secretary had alerted me in advance. Cabañas possesses the aura of a diplomat who knows you the moment he looks at you, like some kind of a mind reader. It took me several minutes to regain my composure under his knowing gaze.

Cabañas, who rarely gives interviews, is trained to listen to questions attentively. He doesn't jump to respond until you are fully done with your questions. In fact, he waits close to ten seconds even if you have finished your question to allow for a pause or for the impact of your question to sink in. This quality of his as a top-notch diplomat—to not only listen but also to assess the person raising the question—is widely known among other Cuban officials who are familiar with his style.

I asked him about western Miami where Cuban exiles—and politicians from among them—form the most stringent critics of the Cuban experiment. He busts the perversely counter-intuitive declarations by Cuban Americans in their early years in the US, having fled Cuba after the Revolution: that they were hounded out because they were bourgeoisie who owned sugar mills and big businesses. Cabañas joked, 'If so many people had sugar mills, then Cuba was a land full of sugar mills and the archipelago wouldn't have had the space to accommodate them.'

He also argued that whenever you look for a job in the US, what sells is the story of victimhood. And when you are asked to fill out forms asking whether you stand for or against Cuba, the exiles, who know well the inimical relations between Cuba and the US, would never hesitate to choose which side of the bread is buttered. 'Many naïve journalists have made a living selling the so-called misery of Cuban Americans without realizing that political game plans also had a role in perpetuating this myth, although it cannot be said that there weren't genuine cases among Cuban emigres. But one-sided narratives of the Cuban Americans' plight are rampant in the US and, as far as I could gather, among foreign correspondents who are forever ready to buy this story,' he said in his deep baritone.

He went on to add that people 'lying to impress their constituency' have been caught in the act. For instance, Senator Marco Rubio was called out by *The Washington Post* for 'embellishing' his family's story by saying his parents left the island after Castro came to power while, in fact, they had left it before the Cuban Revolution of 1959. According to reports from 2011, he had claimed on his official website that he was 'born in Miami to Cuban-born parents who came to America following Fidel Castro's takeover'. He had also campaigned in 2010 stating that, 'As the son of exiles, I understand what it means to lose the gift of freedom.'[10] According to *The Post* report, Rubio's parents had left Cuba in 1956 during Batista's period for economic reasons. Rubio's website now makes no such claims and instead says the following: 'Marco Rubio was born in 1971 in Miami, Florida, as the son of two Cuban immigrants pursuing the American Dream. His father worked as a banquet bartender, while his mother split time as a stay-at-home mom and hotel maid. From an early age, Rubio learned the importance of faith, family, community and dignified work to the good life. Rubio was drawn to public service in large part because of conversations with his grandfather, who saw his homeland destroyed by communism.'[11] Similarly, Rafael Cruz, father of American politician Ted Cruz, a trenchant critic of any rapprochement between Cuba and the United States, was an opponent of the Batista regime and migrated from Cuba to the US in 1957.

In her 1987 work titled *Miami*, Joan Didion skilfully captures the relationship between Cuban exiles and Washington D.C. She uncovers the way Cuban exiles were manipulated by the CIA and drawn into conflicts in Latin America. She began to focus on Miami after noticing the names of Cuban and Latin American dissidents in the Kennedy assassination hearings of the late 1980s. While they were at the forefront of the failed Bay of Pigs attack, the Watergate wiretapping scandal, and so on, they were also indicted in the 6 October 1976 terror strike on the Cubana de Aviación Flight 455 from Barbados to Jamaica.[*]

One such Cuban exile was Luis Posada Carriles. He not only helped organize the Bay of Pigs Invasion, but was also implicated in a series of bombings in Cuba after becoming an agent for the CIA. The National Security Archive in 2006 posted on their website about 'new investigative records that further implicate Luis Posada Carriles in that crime of international terrorism. Among the documents posted is an annotated list of four volumes of still-secret records on Posada's career with the CIA, his acts of violence, and his suspected involvement in the bombing of a Cubana flight, which took the lives of all 73 people on board, many of them teenagers.'[12]

Cabañas reiterated that most Americans favoured the lifting of American sanctions, and even the majority of Cuban-American exiles weren't vehemently opposed to the easing of American sanctions on Cuba. He cited as evidence the Florida International University's (FIU) Cuba Poll, which was first conducted in 1991. The poll, says FIU, is the longest-running research project tracking the opinions of the Cuban-American community in South Florida. It is directed by Dr Guillermo J. Grenier and

---

[*] Cubana de Aviación Flight 455 was a Cuban flight from Barbados to Jamaica that was brought down on 6 October 1976 by a terrorist bomb attack. All 73 people on board the Douglas DC-8 aircraft were killed after two time-bombs went off and the plane crashed into the sea. Several CIA-linked anti-Castro Cuban exiles, among them Rafael De Jesus Gutierrez, a Cuban intelligence officer of the Batista regime turned CIA spy after the Cuban Revolution, were implicated by the evidence.

Dr Hugh Gladwin, faculty members in FIU's Department of Global and Sociocultural Studies. The poll is designed to measure the views of Cuban Americans about US policy options toward Cuba. Some of the highlights of the latest survey (2020) available are interesting. While 'the older respondents, the pre-1995 migrants and registered Republicans' are supportive of isolationist policies and attitudes, 'the younger respondents, Cuban Americans born outside of Cuba, and registered Democrats are supportive of engagement policies'.[13]

It adds that among those who have migrated after 1995 to the US from Cuba, 76 per cent have travelled back to Cuba, while that number is 40 per cent among those who migrated before 1995. Quite surprisingly, the survey states that 62 per cent of the total respondents want airline services to be re-established in all parts of Cuba.

Cabañas noted that many Americans—Cuban-origin or otherwise—are interested in visiting Cuba: 'They don't care about socialism. They want to travel and do business. They want to send in remittances. They want to buy property.' He said that when he was head of the consulate service in the US (2012 to 2015), 75,000 unaccompanied children travelled from Florida to Cuba as a precursor to the thaw of 2015 to 2017. 'Don't tell me you send kids to a country that you are at war with,' Cabañas asserted, emphasizing that notwithstanding the American propaganda and hardship caused by the blockade, people who travel to Cuba see for themselves that Cuba isn't the Cuba they were told it was.

The most remarkable example is Antonio R. Zamora, author of the 2013 book, *What I Learned About Cuba by Going to Cuba*, which is based on his close to forty trips to Cuba from Miami. Zamora has a strange political background. Born in Havana in 1941, he left for the US in 1960 and later took part in the failed invasion at the Bay of Pigs along with other Cuban exiles. He was caught and put in a Cuban jail until he was released after a deal with the US in 1963. He became a US Naval officer and later a lawyer. In 1995, he returned to Cuba to study the country at close quarters. That's when he discovered that his earlier impressions of the country were far from the reality he experienced firsthand.

There was, of course, another trigger for the US–Cuba détente to unravel as early as October 2017: a phenomenon that came to be called the Havana syndrome. The symptoms of this ailment, which seemed to have affected several people at the American embassy in Havana, included 'a constellation of physical symptoms including ringing in the ears followed by pressure in the head and nausea, headaches, and acute discomfort'.[14]

A year later on 3 October, US Secretary of State Rex Tillerson said the country was pulling back many members of its heavily fortified embassy—sort of an impenetrable fortress along the Malecon—and also expelling fifteen Cuban diplomats from the US over Cuba's 'failure to take appropriate steps' to protect American personnel in Cuba who had been targeted in mysterious 'attacks' that had damaged their health. The knee-jerk American argument from the beginning was that the physical discomforts were caused by a sonic attack by enemies. Although Cuba protested that Washington was discounting science in this accusation, the Trump administration went ahead with its plan to snap ties with the Caribbean country.

Seven US intelligence agencies did a years-long investigation in more than ninety countries, including the United States, and finally concluded that it is 'very unlikely' that a foreign adversary was responsible for the 'Havana syndrome', which had affected American diplomats and other officials in many parts of the world.

But by then, all the damage was done and Cuba had to face multiple jeopardies that pushed its economy to the brink.

Cabañas, who has worked closely with the Americans in the negotiations, says, however, that he doesn't expect any dramatic change in American foreign policy anytime soon. He opines that the new policy in place in the US can be described as 'Trump–Bidenism'.

Such confluence of interests across the political divide to enable foreign-policy excesses is not new for the US. In his 2003 essay 'The Logic of US Intervention', American political scientist Michael Parenti explained this phenomenon: 'US leaders profess a dedication to democracy. Yet over the past five decades, democratically elected reformist governments—guilty of introducing redistributive economic programmes—in Guatemala, Guyana, the Dominican Republic, Brazil, Chile, Uruguay, Syria, Indonesia (under Sukarno), Greece, Cyprus, Argentina, Bolivia, Haiti, the Congo, and numerous other nations—were overthrown by their respective military forces funded and advised by the US.'

Parenti further explained that the newly installed, US-backed military rulers then rolled back reforms and opened the countries even wider to foreign corporate investors. 'The US national security state has participated in covert actions or proxy mercenary wars against reformist or revolutionary governments in Cuba, Angola, Mozambique, Ethiopia, Portugal, Nicaragua, Cambodia, East Timor, Western Sahara, Egypt, Cambodia, Lebanon, Peru, Iran, Syria, Jamaica, South Yemen, the Fiji Islands, Afghanistan, and elsewhere,' he noted.

What is remarkable, he famously pointed out, is that in many cases the attacks are directed at 'soft targets' such as schools, farm cooperatives, health clinics and whole villages. Such 'wars of attrition' naturally extracted a terrible toll on civilians and frequently forced the reformist or revolutionary government to discard its programmes. In the years since Parenti wrote his sterling essay, we have seen more and more countries and peoples coming under attack from the Global North in the name of 'establishing democracy'.

Cabañas added, laughing, 'There is a new argument against Cuba now: that we are sheltering Chinese spies. This is a new joke. It is a continuation of the theory of the so-called sonic attack. Like the fake story of Cuban troops in Venezuela, they claim that we have a Chinese spy station. Out of nowhere, you have such a story now.' In June 2023, the *Wall Street Journal* speculated that there was a spy station in Havana sponsored by Beijing.[15] A day later, the Pentagon issued a denial. 'In Congress, on the third day, someone says Cuba has become a haven for Chinese espionage. A bit later, US Secretary Anthony Blinken visits Beijing and they have a nice chat,' Cabañas narrated with a wry smile. Accusations were being made for the sake of accusations, it appeared.

As I heard Cabañas speak, it struck me that even if you viewed the world from an American point of view, the reasons that were given as justification for imposing sanctions on Cuba no longer exist. President Dwight D. Eisenhower had imposed the first trade embargo on Cuba on 19 October 1960 and strengthened it two years later under Kennedy. The complaints ranged from Fidel Castro helping spread communism in other geographies to offering a base for the Soviet Union during the Cold War. Those concerns do not exist now. This was why an economist as conservative as Gary S. Becker of the Chicago Booth School had argued in favour of the lifting of sanctions on Cuba in a 2014 essay.[16] The UN vote also must act as a reminder for the US how antiquated its sanctions are. On 2 November 2023, 187 countries in the 193-member United Nations General Assembly voted to condemn the American economic embargo of Cuba for the thirty-first year. Only the United States and Israel opposed the UNGA 2023 resolution. (Ukraine abstained and Somalia, Venezuela and Moldova did not vote.) Clearly, such repeated international rebukes have not forced the US to change its position.

Most sanctions, many of them unilateral ones by the US, have failed to achieve their purported goals and have instead put civilian populations in hardship. The pattern repeats in several parts of the world. In his book *Busted Sanctions: Explaining Why Economic Sanctions Fail* (Stanford University Press, 2015), Bryan R. Early says, with sarcasm, that economic sanctions should not be viewed as a low-cost substitute for the use of military force. 'In the United States' case, its government's sanctions cost Americans billions of dollars and hundreds of thousands of jobs. Economic sanctions impoverish and often inflict misery on the citizens living in the states against which they are imposed. Sanctioning efforts can also estrange the United States from the countries whose cooperation it needs to make its sanctions successful and drive them to form closer relationships with the state it is sanctioning. These costs accrue irrespective of whether sanctioning efforts succeed or fail.' He writes specifically about the Cuba experience, 'Rather than abandoning their failing strategy, US policymakers have repeatedly doubled down on their sanctioning efforts over the years.' Cuba states that, as of 2018, American sanctions have cost it an economic loss of more than $144 billion. This figure is not vastly different from a United Nations agency's estimate in 2018 that an 'unjust' US financial and trade embargo on Cuba had cost the country's economy $130 billion over nearly six decades.

Conservative scholars based in the US have, however, claimed that sanctions were nothing more than an annoyance for Cuba. American legal scholar Richard Allen Posner claimed in an article in 2015 that it is not as if the US were the only source of a raw material or manufactured good essential to the Cuban economy. 'Or that the US was the sole destination for goods produced by Cuba that Cuba had to export to obtain foreign currency,' he argued.[17] Regardless, he agreed that politics was hurting the lifting of the embargo. He stated, '(T)the embargo was and continues to be almost completely irrelevant. Its persistence is probably owed largely to the political influence of Cuban Americans, who will do anything to hurt Castro's regime and who live (and vote) mainly in Florida, where they form a significant electoral bloc.' The nation's fourth largest state by population, Florida is the most important swing state in the American electoral system.

Well, it is anyone's guess when the sanctions will be lifted given that powerful groups continue to conspire to derail any bid for normalization of Cuba–US relations. If done comprehensively, lifting the embargo will enormously benefit the Cuban people and serve as a boon for Americans, who could access cheaper and advanced Cuban medicines for both common and rare diseases, besides having access to other cutting-edge Cuban technology, products and services.

After all, the foundation for future negotiations is already in place, thanks to the historic détente kick-started by Obama and Raul Castro. The likes of Ambassador Cabañas can offer learnings from the epoch-making peace and confidence-building process for future parleys, just as the likes of Ricardo Alarcón, one of Cuba's most prominent diplomats and politicians from the days of the Revolution, did before him.

After leaving his office in CIPI, I remembered that I had failed to bring up an important question to Cabañas—about one of the biggest challenges in his distinguished diplomatic career: the freeing of the Miami Five, Cuban agents who were arrested in the US while trying to infiltrate extremist anti-Cuba militant groups in Miami (one was released in 2011 and the others by 2014). I felt slightly crestfallen because audiences such as these are hard to get. But later, I read an interview he had granted the *Middle East Monitor* in April 2023 on the subject. He told them, 'Surely the most sensitive experience was my personal role in efforts to free the Miami Five—Cubans who were jailed in the US in 1998 for trying to prevent terrorist attacks against their country. They were convicted in 2000–2001, and it seemed that at least three of them would spend the rest of their lives in prison. In Cuba, they were, and remain, national heroes. We visited them and for several years fought hard legal battles in different US courts for their release.'[18]

He added, 'That experience of going to high-security prisons in the US to talk to these Cubans helped me to understand how insane their conviction was—that of being foreign agents and conspiring to commit murder. Contrary to media reports, there was no mention of espionage in the courts.' Cabañas said he was glad that the whole experience 'was for me a very special one; and although it was an extremely tense and difficult period, it ultimately ended in happiness for the Cuban people with their freedom and return to Havana.'

After my long session with Cabañas, I also realized that I had not eaten since morning, as I had been visiting places and meeting people at a frenetic pace. I felt dehydrated, half-starved, tired and irritable. I asked my chauffeur to drive me to Plaza de la Catedral Plaza where, a few days earlier, I had the tastiest tender coconut water of my life. The seller recognized me with a smile, and without asking, he cut two coconuts and kept them ready for me to have one after the other. The coconuts didn't disappoint, once again. I then headed to La Bodeguita del Medio, the famous restaurant-bar just thirty seconds away from there, which, they say, was frequented by the likes of the late Chilean leader Salvador Allende, the poet Pablo Neruda, Marquez,

Argentina-born French novelist Julio Cortázar and Hemingway himself. It wasn't a pleasant-looking place, but not entirely unacceptable. It had a run-down yet eclectic vibe, crowded and bursting at the seams. The old walls of the two-storied restaurant were adorned with pictures of famous and not-so-famous people. So many dignitaries had signed on the walls that I stopped reading after initially looking for familiar names. Opened in 1942, La Bodeguita del Medio survived all these people and a bomb blast in 1997, which was among a series of blasts in high-end tourist destinations to discourage foreign travel to Cuba. Militant Cuban exiles linked to big businessmen in the community were found to be behind them.

I ordered some creole food—comprising pork, white rice, and something called tostones (which turned out to be fried green plantains)—and mojito, which this place was famous for. A band was playing pretty songs, but people were either talking to each other or looking for waiters to order refills. As usual, I ordered two refills in advance and felt smart about my decision. Although the place was mostly a bar and most people were there for 'liquid food', the solid food tasted good to me, maybe because I was starving. Much more than anything else, I enjoyed the ambience of what can be described in India as a *janata* bar. Unless you have enochlophobia (fear of crowds), these kinds of jolly crowds cheer one up, whether in a football stadium or a Cuban bar. I chatted for a long time with a middle-aged man who offered to teach me some expletives used in Cuba. All of them were in Spanish and I memorized only a few of them, but the one that caught my attention was 'papaya', which he said was local slang for female genitalia! He left shortly, but not before sharing with me the 'decent' word for papaya: *fruta bomba*.

The table in front of me became vacant and a new group of four people, one elderly person, two young ladies, and a young man filled the space in a matter of seconds. Without any hesitation, the older gentleman in a stylish Guayabera, the summer shirt the country is famous for, loudly placed his orders, which included mojitos for him and his companions and a Cubanito for him alone. By now, I was familiar with this cocktail, a kind of Bloody Mary that uses white rum instead of vodka and limes instead of lemon juice—a bartender had advised me to have Cubanito a few days earlier as a morning tonic to fight off a hangover. When their orders came, the old man had his Cubanito first and mojito next. He was fast and furious. Unlike with the others, a waiter kept hanging around near him out of familiarity. Soon, he loudly ordered a refill of Cubanito and mojito for himself, again, reminding me of the now-banned arrack shops of Kerala, which I frequented in my college years in Thiruvananthapuram, where one picked up the art of drinking like a pro by watching veterans.

Mojitos with Cubanitos. Masterful, I think.

The Power of BioCubaFarma

Building a robust universal healthcare system is indeed a great achievement for any country, be it rich or poor. Cuba is known the world over for its forever cheerful doctors working under immense pressure not only in their own country but also in the most trying circumstances in disaster-hit areas that need medical assistance. Internationalism forms the backbone of any such Cuban outreach and assistance.

But the burnished showpiece of Cuban R&D excellence is BioCubaFarma (Farmacéutica y Biotecnológica de Cuba), which comprises forty-six companies, with thirty-three based in Cuba and thirteen located abroad. The major entities, the health ministry officials tell me, are the Center for Genetic Engineering and Biotechnology (Centro de Ingeniería Genética y Biotecnología) and the Center of Molecular Immunology (Centro de Inmunología Molecular). Altogether, this conglomerate of sorts employs more than 30,000 people.[1]

BioCubaFarma, which Ambassador Cabañas repeatedly mentioned in his conversation, enters two kinds of pacts with overseas firms and countries. One is the licence agreement, typically in Eurasia and China, to sell and buy technology, and the other is commercial representation and distribution, mainly in Africa and South America.

'This is the way we operate and we are planning to expand,' says Santiago Dueñas, director of Science and Innovation at BioCubaFarma. We are sitting in the BioCubaFarma office near Rotonda de la Muñeca in Havana. Alongside Dueñas sits Dr Tania Crombet Ramos, the clinical research director of the Center of Molecular Immunology (CIM), Havana, and Dr Maria del Carmen Dominguez Horta, head of the Autoimmunity Group at the Center for Genetic Engineering and Biotechnology (CIGB), which focuses on biomedical research.

BioCubaFarma is designed to nurture specialized research with the units complementing one another. At its companies, Dueñas says, all employees are Cuban. More importantly, they are trained mostly in Cuba, although several of them have worked abroad, thanks to the presence of the institution overseas. 'They (employees) came from our universities and our systems,' Dueñas says, adding that the country's capacity to import raw materials faces enormous challenges due to the blockade from the US.

Dr Tania Crombet Ramos, for her part, is familiar with India, having worked closely with Biocon Ltd, established by Indian billionaire entrepreneur Kiran Mazumdar-Shaw. In the timeline of Biocon's growth on the company's website is a mention of its Cuban connection.[2] It states that, in 2002, Biocon established a joint venture company, Biocon Biopharmaceuticals Pvt Ltd, with Cuban biotechnology company CIMAB S.A. to manufacture biologicals, including Nimotuzumab and Itolizumab monoclonal antibodies. Nimotuzumab is used to treat head and neck cancers. Itolizumab is an effective remedy for autoimmune diseases such as rheumatoid arthritis and multiple sclerosis and is currently being explored worldwide as a treatment to reduce Covid-19 disease worsening and mortality.

'Kiran is a friend,' says Dr Ramos with a warm smile. A medical doctor who specializes in immunology and has earned a PhD, she holds multiple responsibilities in the Cuban government. Besides her position at CIM, she also teaches at the Superior Institute of Medical Sciences of Havana. She is also on the board of several international forums and currently focuses on cancer research.

The US blockade could have spelt death for cancer patients. American drugs aren't available for purchase in Cuba, which was why the country had to move heaven and earth to invest in developing indigenous medicines to save lives. The Finlay Institute (Instituto Finlay de Vacunas), named after Cuban doctor Carlos Finlay, who was the first to hypothesize the involvement of a mosquito as a vector of yellow fever, carries out path-breaking research to make vaccines. The institute, which falls under the BioCubaFarma fold, coordinates research in immunology, molecular biology and applied microbiology to develop novel vaccines and the fermentation processes needed for their production. Cuba can boast of more such drugs and vaccines for rare and deadly diseases, including meningitis, brain tumours, renal carcinoma, Alzheimer's disease and others.

Dr Ramos, however, regrets that several such vaccines and drugs developed in Cuba cannot be availed of by

American patients because of the dreaded sanctions. CIMAvax-EGF, a lung cancer vaccine made by CIM following twenty-five years of research, is known to slow down the growth of cancer cells, stop the disease from spreading throughout the body and ensure a longer life for the patient. According to a report, 'The scientists clarify that it is not a preventive vaccine, but therapeutic, although it has also been used in those with higher risks of suffering from the disease.'[3] Similarly, the VAXIRA vaccine, also known as Racotumomab, from the BioCubaFarma stable, is seen to be effective against leukaemia and other tumours. VA-MENGOC-BC is a drug the country developed to fight meningitis. None of these are available in the US for American patients.

Dr Ramos brings up NeuroEPO, which has been seen as a wonder drug that battles the progression of Alzheimer's disease. Dr Ron Geyer, a Canadian researcher and biochemist, vouches for its efficacy in an article where he writes, 'First developed by researchers at the Center for Molecular Immunology in Cuba, it (NeuroEPO) stimulates red blood cells in the brain. It's a recombinant form of the naturally produced erythropoietin protein (EPO), which stops neuron cells from dying, promoting their growth and communication mechanisms.'[4] The report adds, 'During its first round of human trials in early-stage Alzheimer's disease patients, 82 per cent of those receiving the treatment saw stabilization in their cognitive function. For more than half receiving the drug, cognitive function improved.'[5]

Also in the pipeline from Cuban labs is a drug named Heberferon, which is in the run-up for potential use by patients suffering from renal carcinoma and malignant brain tumours. Cuban researchers have also manufactured a drug made from the wax of sugarcane called Policosanol for reducing blood cholesterol, which could also be useful for men with erectile dysfunction.

An article on the official website of the University of Arizona's medical school rues that Americans have no access to another stellar drug from Cuba, Heberprot-P, which is used for treating diabetic foot. 'Developed by the Cuban Center for Genetic Engineering and Biotechnology, Heberprot-P has resulted in rapid wound healing, 75 per cent reduction in amputations and a longer and better quality of life for diabetic patients treated with the drug. To date, the embargo on Cuba has left the US without access to this life-saving drug,' the article says.[6]

Cuba has also developed effective treatments for skin conditions, including psoriasis. The main drug for psoriasis is Coriodermina, 'a topical, water-soluble gel developed from the human placenta by Dr Carlos Miyares Cao, with a success rate of 84.6 per cent of complete clearing of lesions,' according to a report.[7] It is applied directly to the psoriatic lesions. It can even be used for children and pregnant women. Other home-grown drugs are available to combat conditions such as vitiligo and alopecia.

Which is why Dr Ramos says that American pharma companies are keen to collaborate with Cuba, but the system stops them from pursuing it. A few American–Cuban joint ventures in medical research do exist but uncertainty plagues such ventures.

The success story of Cuban medical research is difficult to emulate, given the difficult conditions in which they work. The only reason why it triumphs is the spirit of patriotism and the sense of purpose of its scientific community, according to the officials I met in Havana. They say they place the social cause of making treatment available to the whole of humanity above everything else, including lucrative jobs on foreign shores.

The proof of making do with less, an attribute of societies that live under sanctions, was never more a life-and-death question in Cuba in recent decades than during the Covid-19 pandemic. Short of medicines and facing a lack of access to antivirals from the American market, they had to dip into their own reserves of research prowess and ingenuity to battle the worst killer disease to hit the planet in nearly a century. The worldwide lockdown also meant heightened public resentment as tourism revenues fell to nothing amidst a shortage of basic goods.

Dr Ramos recalls how the science committee met following the outbreak of the viral disease to create a protocol to treat it. The difference between how the biggest superpower in the world and its tiny embargo-crippled neighbour handled the pandemic couldn't be starker. As of 15 July 2021, the US cumulative case rate of Covid-19 in the US was more than four times higher than Cuba's. More significantly, the death rate was approximately twelve times higher in the US.[8]

Cuba, says Dr Ramos, began by immediately administering either a combination of interferon alpha-2b and interferon-gamma, or interferon alpha-2b alone in patients who tested positive for Covid-19 irrespective of the symptoms they displayed. What they had understood by then was that Covid-19 can trigger a 'cytokine storm'—the term encompasses a variety of events that can result in multiorgan failure and death—in pulmonary tissues through hyperactivation of the immune system and the uncontrolled release of cytokines. Cytokine storms can cause a severe clinical complication known as acute respiratory distress syndrome (ARDS)—something we unfortunately witnessed at close quarters during the tragic Delta wave in India in the summer of 2021, when millions of patients were left gasping for oxygen. 'We learnt that the proper time to use interferon is when the patient enters into the cytokine storm phase of the disease,' says the noted physician-researcher.

The University of Glasgow academic Helen Yaffe has written about the international history of Cuban interferons.[9] The story begins in 1957, when these 'signalling proteins'—that are produced and released by cells in response to infections, which then prompt nearby cells to heighten their anti-viral defences—were first identified by Jean Lindenmann and Aleck Isaacs in London. Later, in the 1960s, a US researcher in Paris named Ion Gresser showed that interferons stimulate lymphocytes that attack tumours in mice. In the 1970s, US oncologist Randolph Clark Lee continued the research.

Dr Helen Yaffe explains that taking advantage of America's improved relations with Cuba under Jimmy Carter, Dr Clark Lee visited Fidel Castro in Havana to impress upon him that interferons are *the* wonder drug the world needed. The meeting had fruitful results: a Cuban doctor and a haematologist ended up working at Dr Clark Lee's laboratory and returned to Cuba with vast knowledge of interferons.

The Cuban pursuit didn't end there. Yaffe chronicles that later in early 1981, six Cubans spent twelve days in

Finland with the Finnish doctor Kari Cantell, who had isolated interferon from human cells. This visit meant that the Cubans learned to produce large quantities of interferons. Yaffe writes, 'Within 45 days of returning to the island, they had produced the first Cuban batch of interferon, the quality of which was confirmed by Cantell's laboratory in Finland. Just in time, it turned out.'[10]

That summer, dengue struck Cuba, affecting 34,000 people and killing more than 180, including 101 children. (On a side note, Cuba later presented evidence to prove that the CIA had deliberately released the dengue virus on the island from the US, though the CIA denied the charges.)[11] At the time, Cuban doctors used interferon to halt the spread of the dengue virus at a swift pace, thus saving thousands of lives.

Over the next thirty-four years, Cuba's scientists and doctors became world authorities in interferons, developing various innovations such as interferon alpha-2b and interferon-gamma at CIGB, which was founded in 1986. In 1988, they came up with the world's first successful meningitis-B vaccine, which was awarded a UN Gold Medal for global innovation.

By the time the pandemic struck in 2020, Cuba's interferon had already been proven to be a safe and effective therapy for a host of viral diseases, including hepatitis types B and C, shingles, HIV-AIDS, besides, of course, dengue. It is no wonder then that the country's medics lost no time in trying it on Covid-19 patients.

The June 2020 paper by R. Pereda and others titled 'Effect of combination of interferon alpha-2b and interferon-gamma or interferon alpha-2b alone for elimination of

SARS-CoV-2 viral RNA' is further testament to Cuban dexterity and insight.[12]

The treatment was tried out on hospitalized adult patients who tested positive for Covid-19 at the Military Central Hospital Luis Diaz Soto Hospital, Havana, during the first wave of the pandemic. The paper explains, 'Patients were randomly assigned to receive the combination of IFN-α2b and IFN-γ (HeberFERON, CIGB, Havana, Cuba) or IFN-α2b (Heberon Alpha R, CIGB, Havana, Cuba).' The paper adds, 'The study execution followed the ethical principles of the Declaration of Helsinki and the International Council for Harmonisation–Good Clinical Practice guidelines. No compensation was provided for enrollment in the trial. Patient personal data was protected.'[13]

The conclusion of the report says, 'In a cohort of 63 hospitalized patients between 19 to 82 years with positive SARS-CoV-2, HeberFERON significantly eliminated the virus on day 4 of treatment when compared to treatment with IFN-α2b alone. However, Heberon Alpha R alone also showed efficacy for the treatment of the viral infection. Both treatments were safe and positively impacted the resolution of the symptoms. None of the patients developed severe Covid-19.'[14]

Cuba also conducted another study in sixteen hospitals in eight Cuban provinces. Participants were patients with confirmed SARS-CoV-2 infection, detected from throat swab specimens by real-time RT-PCR, who gave informed consent and had no contraindications for IFN treatment, according to another scientific paper. 'Patients received therapy as per the Cuban Covid protocol, that included a combination of oral antivirals (lopinavir/ritonavir and chloroquine) with intramuscular administration of IFN-α2b three times per week, for two weeks,' it says.[15] Besides all these, people with comorbidities who tested positive for Covid-19 were given indigenously developed medicines and injections to enhance their immunity against viral infections.

Ultimately, the evidence presented for the therapeutic effectiveness of IFNα-2b for Covid-19 suggested that the use of Heberon could contribute to complete recovery.

The remarkable feats attained by Cuba in biotechnology and pharmaceutical research are appreciated by pharma giants across the world, including in the US, as evident from the euphoria among them to tie up with BioCubaFarma when Obama normalized relations. But it proved to be short-lived.

The fear among pharmaceutical and biotech companies elsewhere in aligning with their Cuban counterparts is palpable, too. 'All American pharma companies are interested in buying our medicines and they are not able to do so because of the sanctions. Pharma companies in other countries also do not want to risk angering the US by signing agreements with us. For most companies, even for Japanese companies, the biggest market for their drugs is the US,' notes Dr Ramos.

The case of a German businessman named Georg Scheffer, who faced endless hurdles in importing interferon from Cuba, is a case in point. According to a *DW* report in 2020, when no vaccine was in sight, Scheffer wanted to import interferon alfa-2b (IFNrec) from Cuba. 'IFNrec, a drug typically administered to strengthen a person's immune system, is usually given to patients with dengue fever, cancer or hepatitis B and C. In China, however, it has been used alongside other drugs to treat individuals who have contracted SARS-CoV-2. The results are said to have been promising,' said the report.[16]

Despite Scheffer stating that he had maintained close business ties with Cuba for years, Germany's economy ministry (Federal Ministry for Economic Cooperation and Development) informed him that his inquiry had been forwarded to the health ministry. Even after following up with the ministry in writing, Scheffer didn't hear back from anyone. That sounds like a Kafkaesque fate indeed. Similar efforts by the Kerala state government to acquire interferon in April 2020 also reached nowhere, as I observed in an article at the time.[17] Close to 45 million people went on to contract Covid-19 in India, and despite a robust indigenous WHO-approved vaccination programme, hundreds of thousands died, and millions were left with long Covid and related complications.

On 9 July 2021, Cuba's national regulatory agency approved the Abdala vaccine, which was named after a play by Cuban hero José Martí, making Cuba the first Latin American country to develop a successful Covid-19 vaccine. The Center for State Control of Medicines, Equipment and Medical Devices in Cuba states that Abdala is 92 per cent efficacious after three doses. At that time, three other vaccine candidates were in the pipeline, including Soberana 2, which the agency says is 91 per cent effective when combined with a booster vaccine called Soberana Plus.

A *British Medical Journal* report from August 2021 places the Cuban capacity for managing even unexpected health emergencies of the Covid-19 kind in the proper context:

Rather than negotiating with pharmaceutical giants or the Covax vaccine sharing initiative, Cuba bet everything on its prestigious biotech sector coming up with its own vaccine against Covid-19. And though the gamble has been shrouded in mystery and met with scepticism, it could be paying off.[18]

In September 2022, a *Lancet* report said that the Cuban Abdala vaccine was highly effective in preventing severe illness and death from Covid-19 under real-life conditions.[19]

Despite such accolades, Cuba continues to face odds as US sanctions badly maul its economy and scuttle efforts to attract investment in biotechnology and other crucial segments. Dr Ramos however is confident of positive changes as the world veers towards massive geopolitical realignments. A June 2023 report by Radio Habana Cuba revealed that BioCubaFarma has signed a joint venture with China. It quoted Dr Marta Ayala, director general of CIGB, as saying that the technology transfer contract was signed to cooperate in the research, production, and development of a product for the treatment of different types of cancer. 'We have JVs with countries such as China, Thailand, Singapore, and even in the US where it is a very complicated process and we received special permission,' Dr Ramos confirms.

'The problem is not ours. The problem is theirs (America's),' Dr Ramos hastens to add. Dueñas smiles in agreement.

The Cubans don't think that, if sanctions are lifted, the entry of Cuban drugs into the US would upset American monopolies because BioCubaFarma would need a partner in the US to enter their markets. 'The latter can fix the prices,' she notes. She points out that cases of sudden deaths of young people following Covid-19 infection are very small in Cuba while it has become a subject of conspiracy theories around the world where people view vaccines and not Covid as the real killer. After all, we used vaccines that we had tried and tested for more than thirty years, unlike those who made new vaccines, Cuban officials state.

Dr Ramos continues to discuss what many of us already know as Cuban 'wonder drugs', such as NeuroEPO, the nasal pharmaceutical solution that can be used to fight Alzheimer's disease and is being tested for efficacy in stroke treatment, as well as the anti-cancer medicine CIMAvax. 'In the US, we are trying a combination of CIMAvax and an antibody,' she offers. Cuban scientists are, however, staying tight-lipped about ground-breaking trials the country is doing in cancer and neurological diseases besides cardiovascular and other debilitating ailments.

Sadly, not many people in the world, especially those who rely on Western media for information, are aware of such Cuban strengths for a simple reason: Cuba continues to be portrayed in a negative light over political compulsions. Unless you are deeply interested in the Global South and perspectives from a wide range of sources, you end up being in the dark about the country. UK-based scholar and author Emily Morris has written succinctly about studies on Cuba that are often clouded by deep prejudice: 'These outcomes have been largely overlooked by mainstream specialist commentary outside the island, a field that is largely US-based and funded, and overwhelmingly dominated by émigré "Cubanologists", as they have styled themselves, deeply hostile to the Havana regime.'[20]

Many Indian businesses, too, are unfortunately under the spell of the Western media. The Cuban officials I spoke to see tremendous interest among Indian corporations to do business in their country—especially companies whose representatives have travelled there. But they don't see the enthusiasm translating into implementation or investment. The Cuban authorities expect Indian companies in the middle segment to invest in their country in sectors such as tourism, the mainstay of the local economy; information technology; power; agriculture and allied fields; and biotechnology, where research and development are highly advanced. They want India to spend on biotech manufacturing.

'To do well in Cuba, MSMEs that choose to invest in our country don't have to spend millions of dollars, although they are welcome to do that; even an investment of $50,000 will fetch these businesses good dividends and the country offers various incentives for foreign investors depending on the sector,' says an official. He understands that Indians are less aware of Latin American markets than they are of other countries in the western hemisphere. Dr Aparaajita Pandey, an independent political analyst, who has a PhD in Latin American Studies from Jawaharlal Nehru University, agrees that the complicated relationship between Cuba and the United States tends to overshadow conversations about the Cuban nation. Pandey feels that, however, the world is now beginning to realize that the island nation has much to offer. 'As Cuba is updating its economic models to attract foreign investment, India is looking at the nation as a lucrative partner. There are great opportunities for Indian investors in the sectors of biotechnology, renewable energy, infrastructure, and tourism, especially medical tourism,' she notes.[21]

However, problems persist. The biggest hurdle, an executive with an Indian pharmaceutical company that had ties with Cuban biotech players, tells me in an interview: 'The lack of a smooth financial (banking) route to Cuba is one of the major hindrances to any plans to put money in Cuba. There are Indian players in other Latin American cities, including big ones in IT.' This is because Indian banks, many of which have branches in the US, do not want to take the risk of the Americans discovering that they are facilitating easy banking ties with the Caribbean nation that the US has put on the 'terror sponsor' list and slapped sanctions on.

It is, however, an irony.

According to my investigation, a few European banks had agreed to play the role of 'middle banks' to ensure a hassle-free banking route between Indian banks and Cuban financial institutions, but then the Indian counterparts did not take up the offer—or are dithering on the issue. Such a position doesn't reflect well for any bank or institution of a country that wants to be seen as voicing the concerns of the Global South. Western allies such as Canada, Japan, Australia, as well as Vietnam and China, have no hesitation whatsoever about establishing a steady banking route between themselves and Cuba.

Certainly, in my view, India can do better than that!

Kiran Mazumdar-Shaw, the executive chairperson of Bengaluru-based biopharmaceutical company Biocon Ltd, which she founded in 1978, offers confirmation that the biggest challenge in doing business with Cuba is burdensome banking transactions. She should know because she had a long association with Cuban biotech companies and had entered into a joint venture (JV) with one of them.

She says in an interview with me, 'When Biocon pivoted from enzymes to biopharma, we were exploring antibody technologies. I had heard about CIM (Center for Molecular Immunology, which is part of BioCubaFarma) and Cuba's strategic investment in biotechnology.' She notes that she visited Cuba in 2001 with her late husband John Shaw to understand the capabilities and willingness to collaborate. 'The visit was most productive as we were able to initiate a discussion around in-licencing two antibody programmes through a JV model that included R&D and technology transfer. Two monoclonal antibodies were identified: anti-EGFR for head-and-neck cancer and anti-CD6 for autoimmune disease. By 2002, we entered into a JV,' says Mazumdar-Shaw.[*]

That was how Biocon Biopharmaceuticals was set up in Bengaluru as a JV between CIM and Biocon to manufacture the anti-EGFR antibody at a commercial scale. 'Biocon initiated a clinical trial in India for head-and-neck cancer

---

[*] According to Mayo Clinic's definition, monoclonal antibodies are laboratory-produced molecules engineered to serve as substitute antibodies that can restore, enhance, modify or mimic the immune system's attack on cells that aren't wanted, such as cancer cells.

and in 2006 got approval for its first proprietary biologic BioMab EGFR (biologics are medicines made using living organisms). Later, the second antibody was developed for psoriasis and in 2014, Alzumab (injection) was introduced in the Indian market. Over the years, Biocon had a profit-share arrangement with CIM, which finally ended with Biocon buying out the JV from CIM in 2017,' adds Mazumdar-Shaw.

As with the decision to finally acquire the CIM's stake in the JV, she says that the capacity utilization of the JV was very low. Once Biocon decided to develop biosimilars, it became clear that this would occupy the bulk of the capacity. 'CIM was given a monetary proposal for acquiring their share in the JV that was found to be very remunerative,' she asserts. A biosimilar, or biosimilar drug, is a medicine that is very close in structure and function to a biologic medicine.

While banking transactions were a problem area, there were no issues as technology partners. The two companies enjoyed wonderful cooperation on all fronts, Mazumdar-Shaw notes, emphasizing that Cuban scientists are world-class. 'Biotechnology is a big strength and despite their frugal resources, Cuba does very well in biotech innovation. They are self-reliant in vaccines, biologics and many of their pharma needs,' she explains.

The 71-year-old Indian billionaire says that, back then, the Office of Foreign Assets Control (OFAC), the financial intelligence and enforcement agency of the US Treasury Department, had given permission for several projects and products from Cuba starting with their meningitis vaccine, which was licensed to pharmaceutical and biotechnology company GSK Plc. 'We too obtained OFAC permission when we licensed the anti-CD6 asset to a US company for unmet autoimmune indications. The asset has jointly developed intellectual property as Biocon redeveloped the CIM programme on a Biocon proprietary platform,' emphasizes Mazumdar-Shaw.

Meanwhile, Kerala had reasons to cheer: BioCubaFarma agreed to help set up a vaccine manufacturing unit in the state. The announcement was made during the state chief minister Pinarayi Vijayan's visit to the country in June 2023. This became big news in Kerala's dailies and TV channels because of the obvious political connection between the two governments, where communist parties are in power. This was certainly an area where Kerala had a lot to learn from Cuba, apart from its excellent higher education credentials. Besides diagnostic tests, medicines and medical equipment, BioCubaFarma also produces, although not in large volumes, diagnostics and pharmaceuticals used in precision agriculture.

For me, meeting such enormously motivated and committed men and women—like Dr Ramos and her colleagues and fellow researchers—at the large entity called BioCubaFarma, which is all about inter-institutionality and inter-sectoriality, was an epiphany. It reaffirmed my faith in the productivity of public-sector institutions. I felt proud to be part of a myth-busting exercise led by the brilliant UK economist Mariana Mazzucato, revealing that many technologies we now credit the private sector for were actually developed with taxpayers' money and primarily by public institutions. This includes the internet, touchscreen technology, search algorithms, microchips, LCD, GPS, memory disks, Apple's voice assistant Siri, and even significant advances in aviation, nuclear energy and biotechnology.*

Several economists and public intellectuals have highlighted this paradox of sorts for decades, arguing that ordinary taxpayers are stakeholders in such inventions and discoveries and they too need to be rewarded with free or subsidized access. But the contribution of the common people is often ignored in a world where tech entrepreneurs and Big Pharma, who flourish on government backing and subsidies, trash such appeals for equitable decisions as theft of intellectual property rights. The affluent classes simply feign that their glory is thanks to their own hard work and brilliance. The great public intellectual and linguist Noam Chomsky has always reminded us that these arguments are fallacious. 'This doctrine is mostly a myth. Most of this work (innovation) takes place in the public sector with public funding,' he has asserted.[22]

I couldn't help feeling excited. Right in front of my eyes, the hyped narrative about the private sector's innovation and high tech that invariably omits the role of the state had gone up in smoke.

---

* In her book, Mission Economy: A Moonshot Guide to Changing Capitalism (page 30, Allen Lane, 2021), Mazzucato argues that the state and public-sector enterprises are great creators of value, a truth that is often brushed under the carpet in the name of glorifying the private sector, which routinely thrives by commercializing public-sector or state-led inventions in science and technology. She states that without ambitious public investment, the private sector would have proved unwilling to invest in areas where the required funding was large, long-term and highly uncertain.

I felt like puffing a Cuban cigar and pairing it with a Cuba Libre, or 'Free Cuba', the rum-and-coke cocktail that got its name from this island nation.

That night, I ended up at La Zorra y El Cuervo, one of the liveliest jazz clubs in Havana, located in the basement of a building near the Habana Libre Hotel in Vedado. I sent my wife a selfie with my glass. She was just waking up in Delhi.

'Working hard every day and drinking hard every night!' she messaged with five or six heartily laughing emojis.

'Don't tell Amma,' I messaged back, referring to my mother, a former zoology professor and retired Kerala government official, who frowns upon my very Malayali penchant for alcohol. But my wife had helped me save for this trip; she was my equal partner in crime. She sent some more emojis and signed off, 'You're really living your Cuban dream!'

Healers of Our Age

Ernesto G. owns his cab. After he hands me his business card, I joke about him being the namesake of the great revolutionary Che. Ernesto has heard this quip so often, that his response has become a mechanical smile. But the Cuban music in his car stereo makes it look less mechanical, and cooler, I would say.

Ernesto's wife is a general practitioner, who, he says, takes care of 125 families in their Havana neighbourhood. The couple are originally from Guantánamo in southern Cuba, not far from the US military base on the shore of Guantánamo Bay, which housed the notorious prison where inmates—most of them detained since the beginning of the 'US war on terror' in 2002—were brutally tortured for years. Those prisoners were not covered under the Geneva Convention because the US claimed they were 'unlawful combatants'.

When Ernesto's son developed hearing loss, the family moved from Guantánamo to Havana to get him treated at tertiary healthcare centres in the national capital.

Cuba's healthcare system, notwithstanding the concomitant shortage of drugs and equipment due to the embargo, is robust. Salim Lamrani, who teaches at the

University of Paris-Sorbonne Paris IV and the University of la Réunion, writes in a 2021 paper titled 'The Health System in Cuba: Origin, Doctrine and Results': 'Since 1959, Cuba has made health a national priority by establishing a public, universal and free system, subordinating economic considerations to the imperative of public health, with an annual investment representing the largest share of the national budget. Based on prevention and the concept of the "family doctor", it has enabled the population of the island to enjoy a level of health protection unique in the Third World, comparable to that of the most developed countries.'[1]

His view is endorsed by institutions such as the World Health Organization (WHO), the Pan American Health Organization, the World Bank, and others, as well as medical journals such as *The Lancet, Science* and *The New England Journal of Medicine*, all of which, he says, have praised this system and 'present it as the model to follow for developing countries, as well as a path to be explored for the richest nations'.[2]

Cuba's infant mortality rate of four per 1000 live births is lower than in the United States. According to the CIA's World Fact Book, Cuba has 8.42 physicians per 1000 people while in the US, the figure is 2.61. It is 3 in the UK; 5.04 in Norway; 3.63 in Israel; 4.64 in Finland; 0.74 in India; and 2.23 in China.[3] Cuba, a small country of 10-plus million people has almost 50,000 medical professors, more than 100,000 doctors, and around 100,000 nurses.[4]

Some other estimates suggest that as of 2023, the figure is higher at 9.2 physicians per 1000 people.[5]

These numbers alone speak volumes about the Cuban healthcare system. Here are more statistics: Cuba allocates 27.5 per cent of its national budget to the health sector, which translates into more than 12 per cent of its GDP (it was 2.1 per cent in India and 6.5 per cent in China in fiscal year 2022).[6] The average life expectancy in the country is above seventy-nine years, which is on par with advanced countries. Cuba, which has literacy levels of close to 100 per cent, is home to the highest number of centenarians per million inhabitants, according to WHO.

Medea Benjamin, an American activist, public health expert and economist who had lived in Cuba, is enamoured of the Cuban healthcare system despite its seemingly debilitating circumstances in the face of American sanctions. She wrote in 2020 that she saw the heroism of the Cuban doctors first-hand when she worked with them in poor and remote villages in Africa in the 1970s. She was a young woman at the time, working as a nutritionist with the UN Food and Agriculture Organization. She speaks of her colleagues being 'good people who were helping to feed hungry children' but also making hefty salaries and living a wealthy lifestyle they could never afford back home. The Cubans were different, she notes. 'They lived simply, worked under the harshest conditions, and earned almost nothing for their services. Their motivation was purely to help people in need. They called it internationalism and said it was their revolutionary duty to repay their debt to society. They quoted Che Guevara: "The life of a single human being is worth a million times more than all the property of the richest man on earth"', she writes.[7]

Benjamin is a rarity. Even Nobel Prize-winning economists of the stature of Gary S. Becker have not acknowledged the Cuban spirit of internationalism—the missionary zeal to treat people who need it the most—and advances in Cuban biotechnology and pharmaceutical testing and production. In one of his essays arguing for lifting sanctions on Cuba, he, however, attempts to compare the incomparable: economic progress of Cuba and Taiwan, two countries in the shadow of great powers.

To begin with, the People's Republic of China (PRC or communist China) wasn't an economic power in the first several decades of its formation in 1949. While there were no sanctions from China against Taiwan, which was a beneficiary of American largesse (in terms of economic and military aid) in the 1950s and the 1960s, there were no restrictions either to invest in mainland China notwithstanding the political differences. Cuba, on the other hand, came under US sanctions within a few years of the 1959 Revolution and they are still in place. Becker was in effect comparing two countries, one boycotted by the US, and the other that was vigorously assisted by it. USAID played a pivotal role in stabilizing post-war Taiwan, and it constituted more than 30 per cent of development assistance from 1951 to 1962.[8]

Now, despite strained ties and heightened technology wars between the US and China, the US is not averse to Taiwan (besides South Korea) expanding its semiconductor manufacturing facilities in mainland China. What's more, Taiwan is one of the biggest investors in China. 'Between 1991 and the end of December 2021, approved investment in China comprised 44,823 cases totalling $198.28 billion.

In 2021, the value of cross-strait trade was \$273.06 billion,' Taiwan's official website says.[9]

Becker goes on to argue in his 29 January 2015 blog post that 'it is time to end the embargo on the export and import of goods and services between the US and Cuba. The Cuban people will benefit almost immediately. This may just be the time when such a move puts added pressure on the Cuban government to end its failed experiment with communism'. [10]

In October 2023, when I brought this blog post to the attention of American economist Professor Richard Wolff with whom I frequently interact, he started off by saying that it was embarrassing to read the post given the big reputations of Becker and American legal scholar Richard Posner. 'Since both were or are advocates of a kind of libertarian ideology, both believe that free markets (trade) are the ideal, optimum economic organization. All government intervention in economies will, they believe, necessarily lead to inferior economic outcomes than what would occur if government interventions were removed. They define socialism as one kind of government intervention in the economy. On that basis, they argue for an end to the Cuban embargo imposed and maintained by the US government to this day,' he averred.

Wolff went on to state that serious problems undermine any persuasiveness Becker and Posner imagine for their articles. He listed some of them:

1. China has not operated an embargo on Taiwan as the US has on Cuba.

2. Cuba has taken an altogether different 'growth' path than Taiwan. Cuba focused on literacy, education, and medical care; Taiwan focused on electronics industries, military preparedness, and so on. Cuba achieved global superiority among Global South nations in what it prioritized; Taiwan was less successful.

3. Taiwan is over twice the population of Cuba.

4. China is the largest source of imports ($78 billion) into Taiwan.

5. The US, on the other hand, is a tiny source of imports into Cuba ($300 million in recent years).

6. Inequality in Cuba is far less than it is in Taiwan.

7. Since 1989, Cuba's major external economic support (from the USSR) has ended and was not replaced. Taiwan had no comparable cutoff nor any of the comparable negative economic consequences of such a cutoff.

Maybe it is now time to move beyond stale narratives and, as Richard Gott states, the process is already underway. Yet to sweep the achievements of Cuban public-sector enterprises under the carpet or to avoid any conversation about them is intellectual dishonesty that needs to be called out.

Notably, Michael Parenti offers us a powerfully evocative narrative to help us comprehend the difference the Revolution made in the lives of ordinary Cubans. Parenti says in one of his famous speeches recalling a visit to the Caribbean after the Revolution:

When I was in Cuba, I was in Escambray, which is like the Appalachia of Cuba.... I met this campesino (peasant farmer) and I asked him, 'Do you like Fidel?' With all our souls, he said. He pointed at the clinic right up there on the hill which we had visited. He said, 'Look at that.' He said before the Revolution we never saw a doctor. If someone was seriously ill it would take twenty people to carry that person because it would take two days to reach the hospital. First, because it was far away and second because you couldn't go straight, you couldn't cross the Latifundia land (large contiguous land owned by a family) because the boss would kill you. And often when you got to the hospital the person might be dead by the time you got there. Now we have a clinic up here with a full-time doctor ... and a dentist comes one day a week and for more serious things we are not more than twenty minutes away from a larger hospital. That is Escambray.[11]

Indeed, Cuban healthcare—which stresses the intimacy between the patient, doctor, nurse and pharmacist, all residing close to each other—has many critics, who argue that the infrastructure may soon crumble because there is a significant shortage of supplies in the most populated rural areas. Well, the impact of isolation and its adverse effects aren't anything any official I met in Cuba ever tried to hide. On the other hand, they were eager for a foreign journalist like me to understand the extreme difficulties under which they continue to maintain the healthcare system, while hoping that sanctions are lifted soon, so that the Cuban people are happy and do not have grievances. As of now, the American blockade has rendered the Cubans unable to secure sufficient pacts with foreign players, and the economic situation is so grim in Cuba that the common people are bound to be unhappy. Nobody denies it in Cuba.

I meet Dr Ileana Morales Suárez, director of Science and Technological Innovation in Cuba's Ministry of Public Health, in an office not far from Revolution Square. When I enter the well-lit and well-equipped yet spartan conference room, she is already seated there along with two other women colleagues. I am served Cuban coffee, and my interpreter helps to translate Dr Suárez's Spanish to English. Dr Suárez is one of Cuba's high-ranking health officials and has taken a break from her hectic daily routine for our meeting. Hers is a familiar face when you research online about Cuban healthcare, and I had earlier read a longish interview of her about Cuba and her work. She was also in the news for presenting before Cuban President Miguel Díaz-Canel a health review titled 'Science in health in Cuba in the year 2022. Challenges for 2023'. It felt good to sit face-to-face with a professional admired by her colleagues for her hard work, conscientiousness and determination.

'Our healthcare system cannot be seen in isolation and instead, it has to be seen in the context of our social, economic, and political realities. To know how we maintain our healthcare infrastructure one must know how our social systems work,' she tells me. Even in the most trying times— the Special Period and now—Cuba never contemplated making healthcare private, she avers, suggesting that's where they, as a nation, come from. The country is on a mission and the government doesn't reduce spending on healthcare even in the direst of economic situations like the one the Caribbean nation is experiencing currently, she says.

Dr Suárez insists that things must be viewed from a larger perspective. This is why she wants me to know that in a country that has just around 11 million people, as many as 500,000 people work in Cuban healthcare and related fields. She reels out more numbers, stating that 70 per cent of the doctors in Cuba are specialists and the rest GPs, and insists that without seeing the big picture, I would not be able to grasp the import of the dream that Fidel Castro had when he envisaged the concept of universal healthcare in the country.

The Washington Post explains the genesis of the medical Revolution following the Revolution of 1959: 'Cuba's healthcare success is built upon its medical training. After the Cuban Revolution, half of the country's 6000 doctors fled and the country was forced to rebuild its workforce. The training system grew so much that by 2008, it was training 20,000 foreigners a year to be doctors, nurses, and dentists, largely free of charge.'

The report notes that even back in 1960, Cuba had sent doctors to Chile to help in the aftermath of a devastating earthquake, and the practice continued for decades later, including in 2005, when Cuba offered to send medical workers to the US after Hurricane Katrina hit. But they were apparently rebuffed. Reuters reports that Cuba currently has around 50,000 health workers working in other countries.[12]

In his 2021 paper, Salim Lamrani stated that 436 community polyclinics and 15,000 consultation centres scattered throughout the country constituted the backbone of the healthcare system in Cuba. 'Each polyclinic caters to a population of 30,000 to 60,000 people and works closely with 20 to 40 consultation centres,' he noted, explaining that a polyclinic offered an average of twenty different services, including rehabilitation, radiology, ultrasound, optometry, endoscopy, emergency services, traumatology, clinical laboratory, family planning, thrombolysis, medical and dental emergencies, maternal and child care, immunization, diabetes care, geriatrics, dermatology, psychiatry, cardiology, family medicine and internal medicine, paediatrics, obstetrics and gynaecology.

His study says that within these entities, health professionals are responsible for the primary medical attention of the population and more specifically deal with the most vulnerable categories of people, namely children, the elderly, and pregnant women. 'The emphasis is on preventive medicine, hygiene, diet, sports, and the fight against risk factors. Prevention is "the cornerstone" of the Cuban health system. Thus, each Cuban family nucleus—regardless of their state of health—receives a regular visit from the doctor considered to be "the guardian of health". This model has notably shown its effectiveness in the areas of epidemiological surveillance and epidemic disease control,' the paper adds.[13]

No wonder then, Dr Suárez asserts, that although the country is not short of specialists, around 55,000 of Cuba's doctors (more than 50 per cent) work at the primary-healthcare level, which is the pivot of the system. 'The consultation centres and clinics are spread all across the country, in the mountains and areas that are not easy to access, not just in the cities,' she declares, highlighting what she calls the specialty of the Cuban medical system. Even those doctors in primary-health centres are trained by virtue of many of them being specialists in handling medical emergencies, she explains.

I can't help but think of my home state of Kerala, one of the states in India with the best health infrastructure in terms of number of hospitals, ICU beds, and ventilators.[14] All this is thanks to what is often described as the 'Kerala model' of development—or what Nobel laureate Amartya Sen describes as 'Kerala experience'—the highlight of which is high social spending in social sectors. It started in full swing under the communist government that was elected to power in the state from 1957–59, which emphasized universal education and healthcare.[15]

The state, in its current form, came into existence on a linguistic basis in 1956. The southern region of the state had prioritized healthcare even earlier. Scholar Prerna Singh argues that the newly formed Kerala's 'political elites developed a single Malayali identity and competed to ensure good service delivery without discriminating amongst different sections of society'.[16] The trend continues to this day. Of all Indian states, the per capita health expenditure is the highest in Kerala at INR 9871, almost four times the national average of INR 2100.[17] It is argued that decentralized governance played a positive role in the robust nature of primary health centres in the state.[18] The former health minister of Kerala, K.K. Shailaja, grabbed international media headlines during the pandemic and was nicknamed a 'Covid slayer' by some, though some others called it 'media sensationalism'. My septuagenarian mother, who was in Delhi in early 2021, pre-empted the second Covid wave and travelled to our Kerala home in late April. This was before the Delta variant hit its tragic peak in the capital city. She insisted that, in Kerala, she would be safer from disease and better taken care of in case things turned bad. With the healthcare collapse in Delhi a few days later, she was proved right.

A 2021 study commended Kerala's response to the Covid-19 pandemic and identified the synergy of 'five major themes' to explain the efficiency of the system: social capital, robust public health system, participation and volunteerism, health system preparedness, and learning from challenges.[19] In 2023, when faced with a second outbreak of the Nipah virus, the state's health apparatus worked with great dexterity, earning praise from The National Centre for Disease Control, a federal body in India, in the way it deftly contained any spread.[20] The state is looking at exploring tie-ups with Cuba.[21]

I ask Dr Suárez about the shortage, if any, of medical equipment for healthcare professionals in Cuba. Her reply comes promptly, 'If you have to understand Cuba, you have to understand it with the blockade because it has been there for more than sixty years and 80 per cent of Cubans are born in the blockade.' Many Cuban officials I have met say that the blockade necessitated more creativity and innovation. Dr Suárez's department works with the biotechnological ranges, including nanobiotechnology, nanomedicines and nanodiagnostics. They also have a medical robotics group, as well as a research wing in regenerative medicine, all of which involve bioinformatics and big data. Yet, she once famously said that she looks to embrace the best of technology except when it creates a physical wedge between the patient and the doctor—a relationship where she feels human touch is quintessential. [22]

'The pandemic, inflation, and economic crisis are definitely taking a toll on the country,' she says, adding that Cuba still manages to supply medicines its population needs the most depending on an annual scientific review. 'We have a basic set of medicines that is updated every year based on need. This basic collection includes over 600 medicines. Close to 70 per cent is made by the Cuban industry and around 30 per cent or so is imported. We communicate with our biotech and pharmaceutical companies what new medicines we need, and if we need to ramp up the production of existing medicines. They then produce the medicines required,' Dr Suárez elaborates.

As with the kind of diseases that are now common in Cuba—which is the criteria that pharma and biotech companies apply before making new drugs and supplying more of existing drugs—she says, 'The top is heart disease; second is cancer, and the third, brain diseases.' The situation, therefore, is not very different from the medical challenges of a developed country.

Smoking, stress and lack of exercise are the most common causes of death in Cuba, she notes. According to her, it is because the country's doctors and leaders place a lot of emphasis on prevention and awareness campaigns that life expectancy is relatively high in the country. 'Thanks to proximity, our doctors continuously monitor anything and everything that affects the health of a person, including pollution, and various lifestyle habits, and then identify ways to prevent diseases that he or she is likely to get in the future,' says Dr Suárez, who herself has been to several overseas missions.

'Family doctors, institutions and specialized hospitals—we have this three-tier structure in Cuba. It is a cohesive unit and a well-oiled network,' she adds. Salim Lamrani's research paper concurs: 'By making health a state monopoly not subject to budgetary constraints, Cuba has been able to put in place a strategy of prevention and fight against emerging diseases such as Covid-19, which has proved to be highly effective, thus allowing the competent authorities to provide quality protection to citizens and to have one of the lowest rates of infection and lethality in the world.' The thrust of Cuban healthcare is to place the patient at the centre of the health project. That is how the country proved that it is possible to provide top-quality services to the population notwithstanding the structural constraints associated with low budgets.

I mention stories appearing in the Western press about Cuban doctors being grossly underpaid and, therefore, exploited by the country in the name of its internationalism. Dr Suárez counters this in a long, spirited response, 'Our doctors travel all over the world because of passion. We always have a strong ethics code. Our doctors are humble people, and it is not money that drives us to work. Our doctors, when they travel abroad, are paid their salaries back home and in addition to that they get a special allowance for working abroad . . . what is important is we have a system that is committed to the core for people who have never seen a doctor before or those who have no way of paying for treatment or are survivors of an earthquake or other calamities.' She says that most doctors in Cuba are equally willing to work abroad and also to serve their people back home.

'Our mindset is not the same as those who see medicine as a professional avenue to make tons of money. Sorry,' she asserts, shaking her head with finality.

Since 2005, these internationalist doctors have been called the Henry Reeve Brigade, named after a Cuban hero and army officer of the 1868–1878 war against Spain. An overseas assignment means doctors earn more money and generate greater goodwill for their country. Not surprisingly, the US has successfully put pressure on right-wing governments in Latin America to force Cuban doctors—who are there on official invitations to fill the huge gap in the doctor-to-patient ratio in those nations—to leave. [23]

When you speak with doctors and the common folk, opinions do cut both ways in Cuba: that Cuba should dispatch doctors overseas to help the poorest of the poor and that the country should mind its own business and focus on its citizens alone. Ernesto G., my chauffeur whose wife is a doctor, is crestfallen about the prospects of her travelling abroad whenever the need arises either in Africa, Asia, or parts of South America.

For the government, though, compromising on the philosophy of internationalism is an unacceptable idea. For the time being, at least. In the past fifty years, Cuba has sent an estimated 400,000 doctors on solidarity missions to disaster-struck parts of the world.[24]

I ask Ernesto G. to take me on a long drive. He drives me through Old Havana, a city founded by the Spanish in 1519. An antediluvian vibe descends.

We drive along for a long while. We return to where we started off and then pass through La Quinta Avenida

(Fifth Avenue). In another ten minutes or so, we are at El Aljibe in Miramar, a thirty-year-old restaurant that was once visited by the late Anthony Bourdain, the iconic food writer and traveller. That is the attraction. Everyone here knows his favourite: a chicken dish called Pollo Aljibe. I take a photo as soon as the food is served. It is said that the likes of Jimmy Carter, Jack Nicholson and Danny Glover (a friend of Cuba who often calls for the US to lift their economic blockade) have been here, too.

For the first time in many days, I decided not to order a cocktail (this place is known for its mojitos) despite the waiter doing his best to convince me.

No means no.

Breaking with the Past

Worldwide and especially in Cuba, several publicly funded institutions have done well, thanks to the enlightened interest or motivation of their employees and leaders. Even so, the socialist world is realizing the importance of 'self-interest' in human progress. It is famously true of China and Vietnam. What is the scene in Cuba?

Private enterprises were banned in Cuba in 1968. Since the early 1990s (during the Special Period) and especially since 2008, however, reforms allow space for private businesses in some small measure to stimulate the economy. But apart from being self-employed workers (*cuentapropistas* in Cuba), people were not allowed to work for a company. Following protests in July 2021 in the Caribbean nation, everything changed, says Professor Silvia Odriozola Guitart, and 8000 private enterprises have been registered across the country. These private units are the kind that could be considered MSMEs—meaning medium, small, and micro-enterprises. Guitart, dean at the Faculty of Economics at the University of Havana (Universidad de la Habana), met me and my interpreter Gabriela at the spacious Protocol Room, located at the Varona Building (Edificio Varona). Before our conversation started, the professor served us coffee and biscuits. Havana summers are hot and humid, much like Kerala before the monsoon. In contrast to the office of Ambassador Cabañas, the air-conditioners were switched on in Guitart's room, much to my relief.

According to the economics professor, who has authored several academic papers on the Cuban economy, the government's new measure to allow private enterprise can help generate more dynamic flows in the production of goods and services. While clarifying that this is not about substituting the public sector—because the state will continue to be the main supplier of goods and services in strategic sectors—these 'additional actors' can expand the coffer or take on specific stages of the production process such as transportation, a section of the hospitality segment (like restaurants) and so on. The logic here, she explains, is to open legitimate income opportunities for people, especially young people, to find individual life projects in this country, create new jobs and reduce informal work, which in the long run means more labour protection.

I ask a question comparing Cuba's decision with Vladimir Lenin's New Economic Policy (NEP), which has been a great inspiration for socialist countries looking to recondition their economies as they try to find ways to cope with new realities. Without commenting on Lenin's NEP, Guitart says that the project of building a socialist society is in no way being diluted.

Shortly after coming to power after the 1917 Revolution in Russia, Lenin and his comrades adopted a policy called War Communism. During the Russian Civil War (1918–20) period, when the country was under attack from both the Americans from outside and those opposed to the Revolution from within, the new Bolshevik government took over private business and nationalized industry under this policy. They even collected surplus grain and other food products from the peasantry for universal distribution. The policy lasted from June 1918 to March 1921, and it led to unexpected economic crises.[1] The NEP was brought in as an antidote to the effects of War Communism that had badly maimed Russia's economy.

In her paper 'Lenin's New Economic Policy: What it was and how it changed the Soviet Union', American scholar Helene M. Glaza points out that socialism, therefore, had not begun on a good note in Russia following the Revolution of 1917, and Vladimir Lenin was concerned about the unfortunate state of the economy and the impact of War Communism. 'His response to the poor economy he adopted and how he planned to improve it was called the New Economic Policy, or the NEP, which got its name from the fact that it was "new", in comparison to the "old" Czarist economic "policy". The NEP was masterfully designed to bring capital into the state, which it did, and to help it prosper economically,' she writes.[2]

She adds that some socialists believed that the NEP may have gone too far with its free-market economic style and may have even taken the Soviet Union into the trap of permanently becoming a capitalist economy, destroying the socialist priority. 'The original plan, however, was to have capitalism in place until the economy was strong enough to achieve socialism,' she says.

Lenin greatly stressed the 'Principle of Personal Incentive and Responsibility' in the NEP. It would mean allowing for free trade among the peasants so that they could keep or sell whatever they preferred after paying taxes, which were assured of being low. In a way, there was a great amount of trust and faith the state had to put in its people, and vice versa. 'There was an underlying fear, as mentioned before, that capitalism would become too powerful and take over the Communist party and that was, of course, taken into consideration,' writes Glaza.

A 2023 study by scholar Gina Viviane Mardones Loncomilla of the Federal University of ABC in São Paulo, Brazil, suggests that the outcome of the legalization of Mipymes (local term for MSMEs) in Cuba is more complex than it appears.[3] While the study verifies that the expansion of non-state management has advantages, it also found that systemic and political-ideological problems tend to coexist for a long time. 'Although the adaptive measures incorporate market characteristics, the local development projects generated by the Revolution still rule the system,' the study notes. In effect, it says, the historical pendulum movement between centralization and economic flexibility adopted by the Cuban regime could be termed 'feasible socialism or sustainable socialism'.

Lenin, a brainiac and a super-theorist, would have loved those expressions.

What the Soviet leader had tried to do was to use capitalism or exploit it to correct the errors of instant communism, which was imported into his country shortly after the end of the monarchy. He slowly started losing control of the reins of the communist apparatus after suffering two strokes in 1921, and his health continued to be fragile until his death in 1924 at the age of 53.

The Russian communist chief's New Economic Policy had its impact across the world. Some scholars emphasize that it had a greater impact on China when Deng Xiaoping forged ahead with economic reforms in the late 1970s that lifted millions out of poverty and catapulted China into an economic superpower. Ziyi Liu writes in his 2019 academic paper on the new era of socialism in China, 'Lenin's New Economic Policy and Its Enlightenment to Contemporary China', that the Russian leader's policy 'proposes' a series of new ideas that various economic components can coexist. 'It is a great exploration and innovation of the theory of socialist construction . . . Lenin's New Economic Policy influenced traditional Marxist ideas to a certain extent and also played a pioneering role in developing socialist modernization with Chinese characteristics,' the paper notes.[4]

They may not call it NEP in Cuba. There isn't any official word of reforms besides the permission granted to MSMEs. But when you visit restaurants, some of which are quite grand and serve expensive imported food, and check out homestays that help ordinary Cubans make hay, it is clear that a section of the entrepreneurial population is making more money than highly skilled professionals. This class of people who are earning more money have their own aspirations and they often travel abroad with their families on holidays that other Cubans, notwithstanding their status in society, cannot afford.

I have interesting conversations with people on the streets, at bus stations and outside restaurants. Most of them are university-educated students who speak English. Curious about the basic amenities available in residences,

I visit a home in Old Havana, a neighbourhood that, I am told, 'has become a haunt for tourists with money to spend'. Three students live here, two boys and a girl. I ask them about the water supply when, after a small meal and a beer, they bring me water in a jug to wash my hands. There is no power supply and so I ask them about that too. The girl answers, 'Those are very delicate subjects, especially the one about power supply. First thing, as you have realized, we don't have uninterrupted water or power supplies.'

For example, she says that where her mother lives in Havana, water is supplied from 5 a.m. to 11 a.m. 'This gives her time to fill the water tanks she has on the roof and other containers. Everybody does this, and everybody tries to save as much water as possible till they get the supply again,' she notes.

Her friend, a clean-shaven wiry young man with a cherubic face, chips in, 'But there are other places in Havana where the service is every four days. And outside Havana, it can be even longer. I have family in Nuevitas, Camagüey province, and they get water every ten or fifteen days. So, you cannot waste water, you have to use it carefully.'

The third student, who is mostly silent except for occasional guffaws whenever I pull their leg with youthful jokes, hesitates a bit before contributing to the conversation, 'Outside Havana, things are very different. My family lives in Mariel, Artemisa province, and the situation there is cruel, in my opinion. They divided the province into sectors, and depending on your sector you have a power cut from 4 p.m. to 8 p.m., 8 p.m. to 12 midnight, and 12 midnight to 5 a.m. So, you cannot sleep, or do the things you should do in the evening or at night,

The Havana headquarters of BioCubaFarma,
the burnished showpiece of Cuban R&D excellence in
biotechnology and pharmaceuticals. It comprises forty-
six companies, thirty-three based out of Cuba
and thirteen abroad

Plaza de la Revolución (Revolution Square) is a
landmark in the heart of Havana. It is simply the
most visited city square in the Caribbean nation

The Embassy of Russia in the Miramar area of Havana. This constructivist building set up during the Soviet era once housed the most powerful people in the country after Fidel Castro. Architects continue to debate whether it resembles a sword or a syringe

Framed photos of Che, Camilo and Fidel inside the Bocoy Rum Factory in the Cerro neighbourhood of the national capital. Bocoy is the maker of the iconic Legendario brand rum

A typical rundown building in Havana—you often come across government offices in such buildings

Tourists flock to El Floridita, a bar and restaurant in Havana patronized by Papa Hemingway, as he is called in this part of the world. His favourite drink is now sold as 'Papa Hemingway Daiquiri', a cocktail of Havana Club rum, grapefruit juice and maraschino (a liqueur from Marasca cherries)

Havana Cathedral, also known as Catedral de San Cristóbal, in the Plaza de la Catedral in Habana Vieja

Señora Habana, a clairvoyant seated outside the Havana Cathedral. Her real name is Adelaida, and she is in her eighties

Vintage cars, relics of Cuba's pre-communist past, are very much in circulation because of the embargo that restricts the import of new brands

A dilapidated residential building in Old Havana

Cuban street art draws inspiration from pagan worship

Embassy of India in Havana

Dr S. Janakiraman, then Indian ambassador to Cuba, in mid-2023, and I in Havana

Entrance to the University of Havana in the Vedado area of Havana. Set up in 1728, it was the hub of revolutionary activities in the 1950s

Dr Tania Crombet Ramos (middle), clinical research director of the Center of Molecular Immunology, and Dr Maria del Carmen Dominguez Horta (right), head, Autoimmunity Group at the Center for Genetic Engineering and Biotechnology, which focuses on biomedical research, with another colleague at BioCubaFarma

Renowned Cuban physician Dr Ileana Morales Suárez (right), who is also the director of Science and Technological Innovation in Cuba's Ministry of Public Health, with colleagues

like cooking, unless you have a gas stove.' He suddenly picks up steam and assumes the role of a conversationalist. 'In the rest of the provinces, it is the same, probably not with the same schedule as in Artemisa, but they do have power cuts very often. Last year, Havana was also divided into sectors for the power cuts, but not now, which is good for us, but because of that, the rest of the country is going through a terrible situation.' The student is light-skinned with curly hair. Mixed-race persons like him are called *jabao* in Cuba. I like the word.

These are well-dressed and cool young people who carry their guitars and books wherever they go. You expect them to spend their nights the way young people do all over the world—party occasionally. But they don't. The girl, the natural leader of the group, says, 'I don't go out much, probably once a month, and just to have a burger or tacos, nothing fancy.'

I asked them whether they ever visit El Floridita, 'No way!' exclaims the girl, and the others laugh off the suggestion. 'A mojito there costs around 700 pesos, and my salary is 4300. You do the math!' she retorts.

So, they don't visit bars or restaurants and instead buy a few beers or rum at private stores near their home where shopkeepers stock drinks bought from what are called MLC stores—stores that use Cuba's official digital currency Moneda Libremente Convertible, or MLC, through prepaid cards. 'The private shops buy beer from MLC stores and then resell them at higher prices,' the students tell me. These prepaid cards accept only dollar or euro deposits and can be used to make purchases from MLC stores. The government floated the scheme to build its foreign-currency reserves after the tourism inflow dried up during the Covid-19-induced lockdown.

Foreign currencies are usually exchanged at official exchange houses called CADECA (Casas de Cambio de Cuba). I am able to use dollars or euros in cash almost everywhere except at government outlets, which only accept CUP. MLC cards can also be used at private enterprises, which have mushroomed since the protests of July 2021.

The second young man, who lived in El Cerro in Havana at the time of the protests, recalls, 'It was a hard time . . . I saw people protesting near my house and heard gunshots. I was sad.' In his essay 'Fidel and the Craft of the World', Marquez wrote that, even in the early years of the Revolution and for decades later, Fidel Castro was deeply worried about the colossal bureaucratic incompetence that affected nearly every aspect of daily life, and most particularly domestic happiness. The Colombian writer said Castro's officials did not want to tell him the truth so as not to give him more reasons for concern than he already had. According to Marquez, Castro told one such official, 'You hide truths from me so as not to trouble me, but when at last I discover them, I will die from the effects of facing so many truths that you failed to tell me.'

Castro's Revolution is facing graver challenges now, and the new generation isn't prepared to be in a perpetual 'sacrifice mode', unlike their parents.

As a friend of the Caribbean nation, I was crestfallen to know that in many local homes, as opposed to swanky restaurants and hotels or resorts that had uninterrupted power and water supply, the situation was similar to 1980s Kerala. There was no running water, and we had regular power cuts—which Indians call load-shedding. Kerala has drastically improved on the power front, but admittedly, most other parts of India suffer from erratic power supply even today.

Byju Sukumaran, my classmate from Sainik School Kazhakootam, Thiruvananthapuram, a former fellow leftist who is now a top-notch techie, has been to Cuba on multiple occasions, besides several other Latin American countries. 'Cuba somehow is arrested in time. It is relatively backward, especially in the hinterland. But some areas are almost unexplored and exquisitely beautiful,' he tells me.

He visited parts of Cuba's southern provinces, and went to resorts in Chivirico, Santiago de Cuba, and Bayamo (the capital city of the Granma Province) among others.

'The resorts are great. They cater to tourists and have all the amenities. But outside the resort, in many parts, there's no electricity, no running water, and a lot of poverty,' he shares.

On one occasion, Byju left his resort and ventured out for lunch at the home of a colleague's family, whose ancestors were originally European Spanish settlers in Cuba. 'The home had fans and lights, but they did not work, and the guy said they get power only a few hours a day. They had plumbing but no water and they gave us water in a plastic bottle to wash,' he narrates.

The enthusiasm and patriotism of Cuban officials and elders are not often shared by the young and those who want to live well. But whether they achieve glory by migrating abroad is an altogether different matter. In my school years, the constant refrain from our seniors was—leave Kerala. Then it became—leave India. Many of those who left the state and the country have done well. But many others haven't, forced to make do with minimal resources on foreign shores.

It is not that the cities in the Global North have roads paved with gold or that extreme poverty or inequality have been eliminated. On the other hand, all over the US, the world's largest superpower in Cuba's neighbourhood, cities are a veritable storehouse of crime, drugs, homelessness and abject poverty. Before I flew into Havana, I was in New York, a city that perhaps exemplifies the inequalities that capitalism breeds. Since 2014, poverty rates in New York have surpassed the national average and in 2021, almost 2.7 million New Yorkers lived in poverty, or 13.9 per cent, compared to 12.8 per cent of all Americans. According to a report, poverty rates in New York's counties varied significantly, ranging from a low of 5.7 to a high of 24.4 per cent and it points out that poverty rates are much higher for children than for adults.[5] Wage disparities, too, are high, and women-dominated professions such as teachers and nurses are underpaid in some US states.

American capitalism is especially harsh on the have-nots and those who did not start out with generational wealth or racial privilege. *The New York Times* ran an article in 2019 about the 'brutality' of American capitalism, which said, 'Those searching for reasons the American economy is uniquely severe and unbridled have found answers in many places (religion, politics, culture). But recently, historians have pointed persuasively to the gnatty fields of Georgia and Alabama, to the cotton houses and slave auction blocks, as the birthplace of America's low-road approach to capitalism.'[6]

Close to two average American lifetimes (seventy-nine years) have passed since the end of slavery. 'It is not surprising that we can still feel the looming presence of this institution, which helped turn a poor, fledgling nation into a financial colossus. The surprising bit has to do with the many eerily specific ways slavery can still be felt in our economic life,' the article posits. Historians Sven Beckert and Seth Rockman, authors of *Slavery's Capitalism* have dwelt on the subject earlier and have argued that 'American slavery is necessarily imprinted on the DNA of American capitalism.' Truth be told, migrants from Cuba who head to the US aren't entering a world where honey and milk flow. Far from it, they start off with a huge disadvantage, as studies show.[7]

Aspiration is a universal sentiment that cannot be bottled forever. But in what was largely an equal society, the new opportunities to grow economically have triggered social problems over wage disparities. After all, risk is built into aspirations. A report in *Al Jazeera* by a correspondent who visited Cuba says, 'The private sector is roaring back, bringing with it more productivity but also more inequality to the island nation.'[8] The reporter met Roberto Rojas, who owns the Rojas Dairy in the town of Güines in Western Cuba and employs twenty-eight people to make yoghurt and ice cream. The report described Rojas Dairy as 'something of a poster child of young, innovative, socially responsible businesses'. *Al Jazeera* quoted a former government employee named Jakcel Conteras, a former vet's assistant who, the report says, is now one of hundreds of thousands of Cubans working in the private sector. 'When I worked for the state, I earned 800 to 900 pesos a month, now I earn between 10,000 and 15,000 pesos a month,' he is quoted as saying.

All this doesn't surprise me. Thanks to my nocturnal visits to many of Havana's eateries and bars, I have been rubbing shoulders, sometimes literally, with the relatively well-off locals employed in the private sector.

At several casa particulares I visited in Havana, I met people saying the same thing: that they are highly educated but choose to give up their government jobs to make more money. A little bit of exaggeration is not uncommon among ordinary Cubans (some of whom also have a penchant for talking animatedly about sex and using slang words for all kinds of people and sexual orientations, as I discover much to my amusement). But certainly, private enterprises help local people make more money compared to the low wages in government jobs. My cab drivers tell me that black marketing is common in Cuba, as it would be in any country that has suffered sanctions and faces a shortage of goods.

I am reminded that in the former Soviet bloc of countries in eastern Europe in the late 1990s and the 2000s one would often come across people who compared the past with the present. Those in public sector employment would say, 'Earlier, we had money but no goods to buy. Now we are spoilt for choice but have no money to buy those goods.'

Experiments with private enterprise do produce inequalities, as is well-known. Cuba has been one of the most equal countries in the world, but that may not last long. The change seems obvious, already, with a new emerging middle class that has greater disposable income.

Unfortunately, being highly educated and qualified doesn't translate to more money here. That isn't good news.

Lenin faced a similar contradiction during his NEP years and looked at ways to resolve it. But before he could do much, he passed away and his successor Stalin, a puritanical Marxist, initiated growth plans completely disregarding self-employed entities. Meanwhile, China confronted the problem on a much more massive scale than Russia did after Lenin's NEP. One of the biggest criticisms of Deng by the radicals within the communist party in China was that his reforms brought in a new privileged class and deepened inequalities as the years passed by.

Two months before Deng initiated economic reforms in China in December 1978, he had made a visit to Japan, where he was stunned by the wonders of technology. He sought Japanese help to modernize China and bring in fast trains, manufacturing bases and improve the lives of his people who had had enough of the horrors of Mao's political interventions that cost lives. The Japanese immediately promised help, and soon Deng received technological assistance. The West became keen on catalyzing China's reforms with the hope that such bids would usher in political reforms sooner or later. Indeed, there were signs of such churning happening and that the communist party would become less and less involved in matters of the state.

An impressive 1999 book republished in 2012 called *China: Twenty Years of Economic Reform*, edited by Ross Garnaut, director of Asia Pacific School of Economics and Management at The Australian National University, Canberra, Australia, and Ligang Song, fellow, Australia-Japan Research

Centre, Australia, features an essay by Li Shi, a professor at Institute of Economics, Chinese Academy of Social Sciences, Beijing. It talks about the growth due to the reforms thus:

> The average annual growth of GDP per capita was as high as 8.4 per cent during the period 1978 to 1997. The Human Development Index also indicates an improvement in well-being on the average for the Chinese population (UNDP 1998). During this time, China has become strongly integrated into the world economy. China's exports grew an average of 16.7 per cent per annum over the last two decades. China absorbed $205 billion as foreign direct investment during the period 1990-97.

Li, however, adds that the transition towards a market economy and openness has not been without its problems. An examination of the distribution of wealth in a fast-growing economy such as China's provides us with an alternative criterion to evaluate its performance, he says, while drawing on two household-income surveys with large sample sizes drawn from rural and urban China in 1988 and 1995.

According to him, economic reforms and subsequent changes in lifestyle have had a significant impact on the equality of income distribution in China. As a result, income inequality has worsened within rural China and urban China, and between rural and urban areas.

Nathan Sperber, a keen watcher of the Communist Party of China (CPC) and an astute Gramsci scholar, quotes in his recent and widely read essay, 'Party and State in China' (published in *The New Left Review*) a paragraph from Deng's work titled 'Reforming the System of Party and State Leadership' to demonstrate that Deng wanted to remove a whole set of missions and prerogatives from the CPC's remit:

> From now on, for all matters within the government's competence, it is the State Council and the local governments that will discuss, decide and issue relevant documents. The Central Committee and local committees of the party will no longer send out instructions and take decisions on such matters.[9]

Sperber, a fantastic scholar whose knowledge of Chinese ways would astound even an insider to the party, traces further efforts to reduce the 'breadth of the party's work' in 1987 under Zhao Ziyang as general secretary. But everything came to a halt following troubles in the Soviet Union, and the Tiananmen Square events of June 1989, when students clashed with Chinese forces, and many were killed. CPC cells within companies, enterprises and boards across China, known as *Dangzhu*, became more active than ever before, calling the shots and shaping policies in every entity in the country.

Coming to Xi's dispensation, Sperber points out that 'the politics of Xi point to a degree of CPC supremacy over the state unprecedented in the regime's history'.

Like China, Cuba knows very well that it cannot let bureaucracy rule while the party reigns merely in name, as it was in the Soviet Union, leading finally to its disintegration. In that sense, for the Cuban communist party, the role model certainly will be the People's Republic of China that Sperber rightly describes as the 'awesome survivor of twentieth-century Socialism's ruination'.

But then, retaining the absolutist party-centric system requires more resources and a sterner sense of purpose than one can comprehend. This conviction lasts only until hurdles appear and demand multiplies, especially from those people who are beneficiaries of the Cuban policy to promote small and medium enterprises. Whether Cuba, another remarkable survivor in more ways than one, will successfully walk the tightrope the way China has so far walked isn't easy to predict.

Now, a word on Cuban enterprise.

Since the Special Period, Cubans have found a way to fight poverty. While tales around Cuban men and women taking to prostitution (female sex workers are called *jineteras* in Cuba and the males *jineteros* or *pingueros*) are a common source of chatter among tourists who often brag about their conquests after returning home, many enterprising locals started running home kitchens to make extra income. Although not legal, these micro-enterprises began to thrive across Cuba, and the citizens began to get a taste of entrepreneurship out of necessity to survive the seemingly insurmountable odds of shortage and economic crisis.

Such eateries—which one enters through backstairs or rear doors—are called *paladares,* and are now legal. According to local lore, they got their name from a fictional home restaurant called Paladar that featured in a successful Brazilian soap opera *Vale Todo* (Anything Goes) on Cuban TV in the 1990s. The protagonist was an enterprising woman who had several tables in her living room, and so she decided to turn her home into a restaurant.

Earlier, paladares were intimate, homely operations—imagine walking into a stranger's living room and having a freshly cooked meal with them for a modest charge—but many of these have now become high-end restaurants. The growth of paladares brought into the mainstream Cuban dishes and the secret cuisines of the multiple ethnicities in the country. I have had the pleasure of relishing food at some such places of gastronomical delight, including the emblematic La Guarida, which—though not as homely as paladares used to be—is still quite an experience. As the saying goes, there are two kinds of tourists in Havana: those who have been to La Guarida and those who haven't (I would say that about many other eateries too). Famous for its celebrity clientele, lively atmosphere and delicious food, its presence in a rundown residential neighbourhood only adds to its exotic charm. Ranked high on most restaurant-rating websites, it reminds me of the happy buzz at most Colaba joints in Mumbai on Saturday nights. The pricing at La Guarida, however, is out of reach for most locals in Havana.

Exposure to the good life among a section of the population, especially in urban centres, means people have become more aspirational than they used to be—that is the feeling one invariably gets in Cuba. Isn't it human nature after all? Although she didn't express it in as many words, I sensed that my interpreter Gabriela was discontent with the growth prospects in her career. One doesn't have to spell it out or talk in a complaining manner to give such an impression. A gesture here, a gesture there, that is enough to decode what young people think of opportunities in their country.

Politically conscious and smart, Gabriela is an artist with words. She is thorough with her work and her job skills are admirable. She speaks excellent Spanish, English and French. And she is enormously attentive. Why wouldn't a young linguistic expert like her crave lucrative job prospects? Having once picked her up from home—which was in the low-income neighbourhood of Lawton in Havana—on my way to interviews with officials, I couldn't help but admire how, in a short period (she finished college in December 2022), she had become a high-class professional working with senior government functionaries. Generally, she comes across as an extremely intelligent and driven person. Most of her classmates have left the country and are looking for jobs abroad, she tells me. I ask her—although I shouldn't have—how much she earns in her job, and I feel sad on discovering that she is grossly underpaid. She has stayed back in Cuba for the time being. But who can blame her if she decides in the future to relocate elsewhere, fully prepared to struggle to find a well-paying job?

When the country wasn't as consumerist as it is now, it would have been easier to stay proud of what you do and about your country, whatever be your take-home paycheque. But no longer. We all understand human behaviour in an unequal society, and I am sure the government in Cuba understands that too. Which was why reforms have been continuous since the early 2010s under Raul Castro (who took on the mantle from older brother Fidel in 2008 and relinquished the post of president of Cuba ten years later). It is likely that he knew it was an unhappy situation. After a round of success with Obama, however, Cuban hopes of normalization of ties with the US hit the skids when Trump won. Elimination of extreme poverty and access to free universal healthcare and education can only take Cuba this far amidst the economic strangling by the West.

Humans are hardwired to chase their desires. No force on earth can kill that urge to break free. Several questions arise now. Is Cuba pragmatic enough to steer through a transition by exploiting the market economy for its own good? Will the communist party feign loosening the strings and allow for reforms to dramatically improve the economy and then tighten its grip as China is doing now?

There are enough indications that the Cuban communist party isn't falling off the guardrails yet. After all, the late Cuban revolutionary and top official Ricardo Alarcón, the political guru of several communist leaders, had taken several steps to ensure that the new generation that is more adept and quicker at making decisions would be in charge. Gott has written about this in *Cuba: A New History* before, saying, 'Far from being controlled by veterans of the Revolutionary War, Ricardo Alarcón claimed in 2001 that the majority of people in the government and the Communist Party are under forty.' Preparations had been on, for sure, to keep pace with the changing times. Havana-based historian Dr Sergio Guerra Vilaboy tells me: 'The legacy of Ricardo Alarcón de Quesada is that of ethical diplomacy, attached to international standards and committed to the defence of his country and institutions. His opinion was precious to the Cuban government in decision-making. But he was particularly radical in matters that had to do with relations with the United States, a topic in which he became the first

Cuban specialist, which explains the trust placed in him by Fidel Castro.' Vilaboy, author of *Cuba: A History*, adds that Alarcón continued to be consulted on everything related to relations with the United States until his final years.[*]

One doesn't need to master nuances of political theory to comprehend that this is a country in transition that still braves the blockade thanks to sheer willpower and ingenuity. Dr Helen Yaffe tells me, 'Right now, the big challenge in Cuba is how they can survive the suffocating blockade and how they can continue to keep the lights on, people fed, hospitals supplied and so on in the context of the tightened sanctions and the impact of the Covid-19 pandemic.' To the specific question on wage disparities, she quips, 'This issue of wage differential in Cuba dates back to the 1990s—I discuss it in my book *We Are Cuba: How a Revolutionary People Have Survived in a Post-Soviet World*. You are asking about rich Cuban Americans splurging money in Cuba but—at a point when Trump and Biden have pounded Cuba with sanctions—coercive measures have slowed the flow between the US and Cuba to a trickle.'

Meanwhile, the lugubrious face of a young woman waiting with her children for the next bus is vastly different from the conviction of the communist party's leaders. Confusion is in the air like the enticing smoke rings of a Cohiba cigar.

---

[*] In 1962, Alarcón was a professor of American History at the University of Havana, a professorship that Vilaboy currently holds. Alarcón was president of the Cuban National Assembly for twenty years until 2013 and was for a long time considered the third-most important politician in Cuba after the Castro brothers.

Vitamin R in Tobacco Land

Maritza, the travel manager of the Nacional Hotel, books me on a one-day bus tour of the western part of the island nation. Never an admirer of these touristy trips, I choose this one because it is the best way to visit the country's most famous tobacco-growing area. I have already bought three expensive single cigars from tobacco sellers that Alex the chauffeur had taken me to in Havana—one an H. Upmann Magnum 56 limited edition, a Cohiba Lanceros (which was the cheapest of the Cohiba brands I could lay my hands on in the capital city) and a Montecristo Edmundo, which is named after Edmund Dantes, the hero of the Alexander Dumas's novel *The Count of Monte Cristo*. All these are for a Malayali friend, who is a cigar aficionado. I plan to buy more cigars for other friends when I visit the tobacco farms.

A non-smoker, I wouldn't have taken interest in Pinar del Río had it not been for its culture and reputation for making some of the finest cigars in the world—and the realization that cigars mean a lot for the government of Cuba. It exports cigars to most parts of the world, except the US where it cannot sell its cigars or rum or for that matter any of its homegrown products. It is an altogether different matter that Americans still manage to smoke Cuban cigars.

The American tourists I met in Cuba told me their biggest draw was cigars and rum. Many of them had booked return flights via other countries and made sure that they peeled off the packaging in case customs officers checked for Cuban goods when they landed back home.

Located more than 160 kilometres from Havana, Pinar del Río is Cuba's western-most province and is well-known for a UNESCO world heritage site called El Valle de Viñales (Viñales Valley) and the tobacco-growing region of Vueltabajo.

On our way in a luxury Yutong bus, I notice that most of the tourists are from Canada, the Caribbean and Spain, and one each from India, US and Japan. The American is accorded much warmth by our guide, who says she is glad to see him as part of this team, and that since it is his first visit, she will make sure he gets to speak with as many local people as possible.

It is a long drive on A4, a six-lane motorway built with Soviet and East European assistance. The terrain, foliage and trees all around look no different from southern India except for the roads and the vehicles that we overtake. There isn't much traffic. I merrily click photos of old, comic-looking cars, some of which are, as writer and journalist Anthony DePalma describes them, ugly hunks of battered metal, held together by wire and running on hope. Certain vehicles even remind me of improvised vehicles one sees in the villages of north India, in which a handset generator is used to fuel what appears to be a cross between a scooter and a bullock cart. As in rural India, one can see farmers seated with their perishable produce along the roads—they are mostly villagers from the Artemisa Province, which includes municipalities such as San Cristóbal and others. We meet several farmers along the route. There are also cheese farmers, those who sell homemade cheese and guava bars. A few cars stop to make purchases, though our bus doesn't. If the driver or the guide had ordered a halt, I am sure many people on the bus would have bought cheese bars. Instead, we drive on, wondering what they must taste like.

The guide keeps making announcements in English and Spanish; she is well-versed in the history of the region. We stop midway for snacks, and I find the restaurant bar to be excellent as it caters exclusively to foreign tourists.

On reaching Pinar del Río, where 65 per cent of Cuba's tobacco is produced, we go straight to a tobacco firm where we are welcomed by a cheerful man wearing a straw hat and clothed in fashionably torn blue jeans and a double-pocket Cuban shirt with a logo of his tobacco brand above the right pocket: Macondo, a farm where tobacco is grown using traditional methods. He holds a small plastic container in his left hand and a brochure in his right. I think I hear him say his name is Nelson, but I could be wrong. He gestures liberally with his right arm, explaining what the traditional method of tobacco farming is all about. He explains first in English and then in Spanish with tremendous flair and a sense of humour, without sounding one bit mechanical or in automation mode.

We are standing in front of a house-cum-barn behind which he will demonstrate to us how to roll tobacco leaves and make a cigar—and how to smoke it. To the left of the house, there stands a barn with thatch roofing made of hay (the house bears a stark resemblance to old homes in Kerala and some parts of India that have thatch roofing using hay and dry vegetation; in Kerala, besides straw, we also use palm leaves and water reeds). Inside the barn, processed tobacco leaves are hung to dry. Once dried, the leaves are typically cured in a special concoction that includes guava leaf, honey and rum mixed into water, a practice that requires great mastery.

I feel as though I am in a Kerala countryside, rich with palms and banana trees and houses made with hay and reed roofs. In the distance are a few buffaloes feeding on grass, and pigs foraging peacefully. The place is lush green and relatively desolate.

After exchanging pleasantries and asking each one of us to introduce ourselves, Nelson seats himself at a high table of sorts, with photographs of Fidel, Che and Camillo puffing at cigars behind him. Also on display are a flag of Cuba, a lantern, and a calendar-shaped figure of the tobacco plant detailing various parts, making it look like a botany lab.

We are served black coffee immediately and Nelson stands for a while behind the handless chair as if he is going to give a speech. He is a natural—confident and full of life. He speaks eloquently, switching between English and Spanish with the skill of a matador in a bullfight.

Then he sits down. On the table in front of him, there is a board to roll tobacco. A vial of honey is placed next to it. So are a few cutting tools, which he touches like a surgeon checking his equipment before an operation.

We are getting into the most important part—how to roll a cigar.

'The first thing you have to do (he translates this into Spanish, too) is to remove the midrib of the leaf,' he says and does so without even appearing to do it. I see the midrib only when he flaunts it. The leaf appears untouched and unaffected by what he has done: this, for sure, is the equivalent, from the leaf's viewpoint, of a massive laminectomy. But it looks as it was before. This is getting entertaining and that is exactly what our host intends.

'According to various studies and statistics, 99 per cent of the nicotine is concentrated here,' he says, brandishing the midrib. 'Have you heard that cigars are less addictive than cigarettes? One of the reasons is this one,' he asserts, referring to the removal of the midrib.

Our man demonstrates his rolling skills along with his bilingual deftness.

'Another reason is that we don't inhale the smoke,' he says, contorting his face to give the expression that it is taboo to inhale smoke while enjoying your cigar.

Then he explains how to smoke the cigar. You roll the smoke inside your mouth, take in its flavour and exhale.

'Smoking a cigar is like drinking wine partly because of the wine you drink,' he avers, suggesting that he is referring to the fun of it, in a literal sense.

He wipes his forehead with a handkerchief that looks tiny for his face.

Then he dwells on what happens to the midribs, or as he calls it, the veins. 'We don't throw them away. We put them in water for some fifty or sixty days. The water gives out a strong smell and we spray it in the tobacco fields. It is to protect the plants against the caterpillar, which loves to eat the leaves.'

He then goes on to remove veins from two more leaves and then starts rolling the cigar.

'What am I doing here?' he asks like a teacher does with schoolkids. 'Tell me what am I doing here?' he repeats himself, in English and Spanish.

Someone mumbles inaudibly. 'Sorry,' he says loudly. 'But what am I doing with the leaves?' he asks again, this time in a harsher tone, rolling his sleeves. One of the guests gets up and sits close to him.

'Yes, you said it,' he tells a lady at the back. 'You are right, I am mixing the leaves. You are right. I am blending,' he says, stressing the blend part. BLAANDing, yes, he says.

'The second part is binding. Holding them together.'

I try to imitate him with my own set of leaves but fail.

'We roll the cigar with the middle leaves of a plant— which are the best for rolling. Then you have to massage the cigar to shape,' he offers, adding that if you know how to massage you can roll a cigar. 'That is why they say the wives of those who roll cigars are always happy,' he chuckles.

Then comes the cutting part. He applies a little bit of honey to make the roll stick tighter. 'This works differently with machines, but we don't use them.'

The cigar is ready for use.

He offers a handful of cigars to the guests. A few people accept them and imitate him—the way the cigar is lit and smoked without inhaling.

'If you want, you can dip the cigar in honey and light it, for flavour,' says Nelson.

Now it is time for sale.

Details about the 'draw' and quality of organic tobacco are discussed. I buy two. He packs them for me with great care. There are many more buyers.

I had once read about the interesting link between tobacco and reading habits—a story that's true of Kerala too. For my master's thesis, I examined how a Marxist newspaper played a role in the dissemination of information among beedi workers in Kerala. My paper was set in 1990s Kannur, my hometown, when the rolling of beedis—thin cigarettes made with beedi leaves—offered a route out of poverty for hundreds of otherwise unskilled labourers. I zoomed in on Kerala Dinesh Beedi, a cooperative run by thousands of workers and a Marxist bastion, which has now diversified into food processing, textiles and so on.

Back then, as the workers slogged on at such beedi-rolling enterprises, they typically hired young students—or someone literate enough—to read newspapers aloud to keep them all abreast of the news. The reader's reward would be a packet of beedi and a cup of tea. If the reader was a beedi worker, others, both men and women, would contribute a share of their rolled beedis to ensure that he or she met the day's work target. I have come across beedi units where they got readers to read aloud novels and other books, ranging from those by politicians of the stature of E.M.S. Namboodiripad and novelists such as French icon Albert Camus and Mexico's Juan Rulfo (all in Malayalam translation). Many beedi workers later became political leaders in Kerala's communist parties.

In Cuba, too, a similar practice is deeply entrenched among cigar rollers. They have very professional readers who read books for the employees of cigar factories. It is a well-documented aspect of Cuban cigar factories, and a practice that has been in place since 1865, when workers at the El Fígaro factory in Havana picked a colleague to read to them as they rolled.[1] The reader was promised more cigars to compensate for his missing hours. Later, the others chipped in to pay the reader a salary. Despite initial resistance from factory owners, the practice spread. It is said that independence hero José Martí himself once sat in the reader's chair to deliver a speech to emigrant Cuban tobacco rollers working at a factory in Florida. The Cuban government has declared the readers' job a 'cultural patrimony of the nation'.

Interestingly, both in Cuba and Kerala, where communist parties hold great sway in the cultural space, the quest for political literacy appears insatiable, especially among the working classes.

For Cuba, tobacco is one of its main sources of export revenue. The country sold tobacco worth $568 million in 2021, which was 15 per cent more than a year earlier. The Cuban government procures 90 per cent of all farmers' produce and pays a 'set price' for it. The farmers are usually able to turn a profit, but sanctions have hurt them, too, especially in years when supplies of fertilizers and pesticides are low.

Incidentally, in 2022, Cuba won a twenty-five-year-old legal tussle over US trademark rights to its famed Cohiba cigars. State-owned Tabacuba, or Grupo Empresarial de Tabaco de Cuba (Union of Tobacco Companies of Cuba), is the dominant cigarette manufacturer in Cuba and a 100 per cent state-owned entity. It has collaborations outside the country through its ventures. The irony is that although Cuba has the right over its cigar brands, including Cohiba in the US, it cannot sell them there because of the embargo. 'They hate everything made in Cuba, especially in Miami', an official had forewarned me before I returned to India via US and Canada. I didn't take it seriously and paid a price for it.

More on that later.

We are now headed to Viñales Valley through the typical tourist route every visitor to this part of Cuba takes. I go through the usual aspects of a touristy outing: lunch, lunchtime drinks, and a visit to the La Cueva del Indio (Indian Cave), which has an underground lake where you roam around in a boat. I feel good and mobile here because I had skipped Vitamin R (that is what they call rum) and had plain, non-alcoholic Pina Colada, not one, but two.

Here, after many days, I miss my family back home. They would have enjoyed this. It is a holiday tailor-made for families. I also miss my trekking friends in Sikkim, in India's North-East, who would have loved the chance to hike in the beautiful mountains here.

But then, I am on my own and I will do it the way I please. Tonight, I will honour my instant friend Enrique and stay back on the lawns of the Nacional de Cuba Hotel and eat at the Cuba restaurant, which serves some mouth-watering items, including cassava (similar to Kerala's very own kappa, or tapioca, which goes with any meat dish); Ropa Vieja (shredded beef) and Moros y Cristianos (Cuban version of rice and beans).

Long before we return to Havana, I am already there in my mind. The lone Japanese girl on the bus, who had travelled to Cuba from Bogota, Colombia, where she is a student of Spanish at Bogota University, is keen to speak about her holiday in Rajasthan, western India. She is in her early twenties and has already travelled half of the world. I engage her in conversation for a while, but soon I become distracted for no special reason other than an overwhelming desire to reach Havana and crash in my bed. It isn't a pleasant feeling but the only thing that makes me feel good is the new stock of Maconda cigars from Pinar del Río, and Guantanamera cigars (along with a cigar cutter) that I picked up from a souvenir store at the Mural de la Prehistoria (prehistoric mural) on the wall of the Pita mogote (hill) in Sierra de los Órganos, four kilometres west of the Viñales town. This mural, completed in 1964 and considered the largest in the world, is a tribute to the first inhabitants of the Cuban archipelago and is one of the most visited tourist spots in Cuba.

When the bus finally drops me at Hotel Nacional, I feel bad about disappointing the curious Japanese girl studying Spanish in Bogota by going silent midway through our conversation. But I am too tired to feel a sense of guilt. I tip the guide—who smiles back heartily—and dart into the hotel lobby, taking long strides towards the early twentieth-century room-sized lift of the heritage building to my room. As it always happens, long bus trips make me sick. My stomach has expanded. I feel uneasy. I want to clean up and rest and, so long as I can stay awake, re-watch Sara Gómez's *De Cierta Manera* on Mubi (by fast-forwarding it for scenes that, I believe, offer newer insights about Cuba).

Che Guevara's Undying Spell

Amidst what Richard Gott describes as the 'selective nationalist nostalgia' and embrace of 'heritage culture' that is there for all to see in Cuba, there is one figure who towers above all others.

To begin with, he isn't even Cuban. But he was, according to most founder-members and guerrilla fighters of the Revolution and later, the only one who originally championed the cause of communism with Latin American characteristics (although he had not given it any nomenclature, he re-read Marx and distanced himself from the Soviet methods). One of his former comrades who had often found him arrogant—as Argentinians often are in his view—concedes, however, that Che was the only leftist revolutionary among the pack. This is the primary reason why, lately, newspaper after newspaper in the West makes it a point to stress that his ideals are losing ground in Cuba. From CIA memos to documentaries, there has invariably been a deliberate thrust on proving, not with great success, that the Guevara era is long over.

But if you look closely and consult serious academic literature, it is easy to find that Che Guevara isn't losing ground at all. The outcome of his work, while in power, is still being felt, except that typical Cubanologists don't have time for a subject they assume is marginal, which couldn't be further from the truth. You realize it the moment you examine pathbreaking research work. First, Guevara is the most admired person in the country, perhaps much more than even Castro. Globally, decades after he became a poster boy of internationalism and guerrilla warfare and notwithstanding concerted efforts to demonize him as a sadist who mistreated his prisoners (often based more on hearsay than any information from primary sources), he continues to be revered much more than any other leader of the Cuban Revolution—even inside the country, not to talk of the rest of Latin America or the Global South. What makes him unique is his unsurpassable appeal as an iconic revolutionary who died fighting. Studies suggest that he exerted a galvanizing influence on Cuba although few people talk about it—instead, they have internalized it. The same cannot be said of other leaders of the Revolution with the probable exception of Castro and Camilo Cienfuegos. But then, Guevara alone has an international halo as a revolutionary and not the head of a regime. Like Cienfuegos who died at age twenty-seven when his plane vanished over the sea near the Straits of Florida, Guevara's early and mysterious death, aged thirty-nine, has added to the mystique around him notwithstanding ideological setbacks to his ideals.

It is in one of those lazy evenings at the Nacional when I am fighting off insomnia that I come across Dr Helen Yaffe's stimulating book *Che Guevara: The Economics of Revolution* on Che's role beyond being a revolutionary, who went across continents and countries with the hope of exporting revolutions.[1]

We have dwelt on Dr Helen Yaffe and her studies on Cuba before. But this book focuses on the legendary leader's legacy as the minister for economy and as a banker besides his role in institution-building, which had a positive impact on the Cuban people, an aspect of Che's brilliance that I, a Cuba buff, have never come across. In fact, the opposite is true: I have heard a section of leftists say that Che wasn't interested as much in governance and nation-building as he was in forging ahead with creating conditions for revolutions.

UK-born Yaffe, who lived with her sister in Cuba during the Special Period, describes her experience of writing the book and the insights she had gained from her research. She writes of her six years of investigations and uncovering new archival material, 'including the internal transcripts of the bimonthly meetings in the Ministry of Industry headed by Che from 1961 and his critical notes on the Soviet Manual of Political Economy, predicting the return of capitalism to the socialist bloc; a document so controversial that it was kept under lock and key for 40 years'.[2] She also shares that she interviewed fifty of Che's closest colleagues and *compañeros* (comrades), some of whom had never spoken on record about their experiences of working with Che while he was President of the National Bank, head of the Department of Industrialisation, and Minister of Industries between 1959–65.

The impression one easily gathers from her book, which relies largely on primary sources, is that Guevara understood the need for argument, believed in the importance of critiquing while still being a politician, and placed human capabilities above the tools often prescribed by capitalism, notably, voluntary work and consciousness. This is perhaps why Cubans understood him well, although certain aspects of his versatility and genius were largely ignored or remained unknown in the English-speaking world.

Like Yaffe, I too can feel the omnipresence of Che Guevara on the island, and it is clear, as Yaffe says, that Cubans recognize him as 'a more multifaceted individual than the one caricatured outside the island; the romantic guerrilla fighter with idealistic notions of how human beings are motivated and how social change is brought about'.

When, in the mid-1980s, Cuba pulled back from the Soviet model of socialism, entering a period known as 'Rectification', there was a return to Che's ideas, approach and symbolism. Yaffe refers to two Cuban academics, Fernando Hernandez Heredia and Carlos Tablada, who provide the theoretical basis for this move—'linking Che's promotion of voluntary labour and consciousness to his Marxist analysis of capitalism and his critique of the Soviet system, which had relied on capitalist tools to build socialism,' she notes.

All this is certainly a new disclosure for Marxists back home in India and Kerala, where I have never come across any book that goes beyond capturing the revolutionary zeal of the Argentine-born revolutionary whose commentaries on internationalism we all treated like gold dust.

The Cuba of the 1960s was a nation in transition going through a tumultuous time—nationalism was underway, as was the shift in trade to the socialist bloc. At the same time, the US blockade led to its own set of issues, including the exodus of professionals, attacks from US-sponsored agencies, sabotage and the real risk of nuclear war. In such a period, Yaffe looks beyond Guevara's revolutionary appeal alone, and studies his natural abilities as a nation-builder. 'Under Che's leadership, Cuban industry stabilized, diversified and grew—testimony to his capacity for economic analysis, structural organization and the mobilization of resources, both human and material,' she writes. Che's approach, she says, was not only based on his study of Marx's analysis of the capitalist mode of production, but also his engagement with socialist political economy debates and his understanding of the managerial and technological advances of capitalist corporations.

As Minister of Industries, Guevara set up nine research and development institutes in Cuba and had a large role to play in the mechanization of the sugar harvest and the sugar derivatives industry. He also laid the groundwork for nickel production, green medicine, oil exploration, the chemical industry and even computing and electronics. 'He integrated psychology as a management tool, secretly organized the printing of new banknotes, devised a new salary scale, and promoted workers' management, inventions and innovations. In six tumultuous years, Che made an indelible contribution to Cuban development,' Yaffe writes.

Gott, who knew Guevara very well and who was in Bolivia when the revolutionary leader was captured and killed, has, of course, written about the dead leader's multi-faceted personality. 'Guevara was not himself an economist but a brilliant autodidact with definitive views about the need for Cuba to escape from the economic embrace of "imperialism" . . . He wanted the island to escape from the tyranny of sugar and to develop an independent economy based on industrialization,' Gott writes, noting that the early years of the Revolution were characterized by an earnest discussion about all kinds of questions. The scholar stresses that, although programmes didn't do well because of multiple concerns, including logistics and non-availability of American machines, Guevara argued that 'industrialization was the only true basis for a socialist economy'.

In an intelligence memorandum titled 'The Fall of Che Guevara and the Changing Face of the Cuban Revolution' and released by the CIA's Directorate of Intelligence on 18 October 1965, there are many observations about Guevara which—although not meant to portray him in a good light—help us understand him better.[3] It reveals that Guevara had heated debates with fellow comrades and ministers on various subjects, especially the economy and foreign policy. The CIA, however, tries to project his opposition to Soviet models and suggestions as proof of his affinity for China. Nonetheless, some of the statements from this memorandum approved for 'limited official use' put a spotlight on the ways and eccentricities of the leader who did not hesitate to air his opinions in public and even write articles challenging his colleagues in government.

The memorandum also states that Castro's 'willingness' to 'drop' Guevara confirms the shift in Cuban policies that it says had been underway since 1964. 'Guevara's fall from power apparently resulted from his persistent opposition to the practical policies recommended by the Soviet Union,' says the CIA memorandum. (On a side note, the CIA's emphasis on 'practical policies recommended by the Soviet Union', a country considered America's enemy, does, in hindsight, evoke some laughter.)

The CIA paper—which appears to deride Guevara for insisting on diversification of agricultural production and increased investment in industry to free Cuba from 'economic enslavement' by the US—quotes various instances of Guevara calling out top-notch Cuban officials for thinking in terms of 'classical economics' and 'vulgar economics'. It also states that Guevara objected to the Soviet proclivity for leaving individual factories to support themselves, and instead, he stressed on centralization to help them grow rapidly.

He wanted each country to formulate policies that best solved their economic problems. In his interview in 1964 with journalist-activist Josie Fanon, wife and collaborator of the legendary political philosopher and psychiatrist Frantz Fanon, Guevara said that it was impossible to give a general formula for economic development to different countries and continents. Responding to a question about the economic development of Africa, he said, 'I would say simply that a country beginning to develop itself must, in the first period, work, above all, at organization and that one should approach the practical problems by "using your own head".' Guevara was opposed to any one-size-fits-all approach. He said in the same interview, which appeared in *Révolution Africaine*, a publication of the Algerian revolutionary movement FLN, 'In a country on the road to development, most problems involve agriculture and extractive industry, but it is quite evident that these problems are posed in a different way in each country, and that one must pay attention above all to particular realities.'[4]

At a time when capitalism is going through endless crises, Guevara's thoughts on economics—much more than his internationalism—deserve to be reviewed. Even Nobel Prize-winning economist Angus Deaton has lashed out at the brightest minds in economics for not serving society but other interests in his book, *Economics in America: An Immigrant Economist Explores the Land of Inequality*. In such a context, efforts such as Guevara's to place the poorest of the poor as central to his policies and his farsightedness must be brought to the fore and debated. This is what Yaffe writes in praise of Guevara's visionary outlook: 'Che's promotion of voluntary labour and his emphasis on consciousness were not idealism but part of the search for ways to undermine the law of value, moving away from capitalist mechanisms in the construction of socialism.'

We in Kerala assume we know so much about Che Guevara whose life and times have been widely documented. But we realize, thanks to stellar works by a precocious new generation of scholars, that we know very little about him. Though Guevara tried to persuade socialist nations to replace capitalist mechanisms by offering them alternative policies, his warnings were not heeded and eventually, capitalism returned to all those countries. 'In Cuba, his analysis was revisited in the mid-1980s in the period known as Rectification, which pulled the island away from the Soviet model before it collapsed, arguably contributing to the survival of Cuban socialism,' says Yaffe.[*]

---

[*] In their 2010 work *Cuba: A History*, Sergio Guerra Vilaboy and Oscar Loyola Vega, both historians, talk about this period of Rectification as one that threw up existential threats for Cuba. 'One of the most serious problems the Revolution ever had to confront arose: the arrest and later trial in mid-June 1989 of several high-ranking officers of

Guevara also believed, avers Dr Michelle Paranzino, author of *The Cuban Missile Crisis and the Cold War: A Short History with Documents*, that the most salient divisions were not between the capitalist and communist blocs, but between the Global North—the industrialized economic powers, including the Soviet Union and other highly developed economies of the Eastern bloc—and the Global South. 'The latter term was understood as including not only the peoples of Africa, Asia, and Latin America—in other words, the decolonising world—but also the subject peoples within the industrialized countries, particularly African Americans in the United States,' she writes.

And yet, I return to Che the revolutionary, whose many sides are yet undiscovered. None less than Garcia Marquez wrote about Che Guevara's decision to leave Cuba on 25 April 1965 to fight the guerilla war in the Congo, which points as much to the intensity of the Cuban presence there as to Guevara's own internationalism. After submitting his farewell to Fidel Castro, Guevara relinquished his rank of commander and other functions in the government. Marquez writes in an essay titled 'Operation Carlota':

---

the Revolutionary Armed Forces and of the Ministry of the Interior,' they write in the book. Among these officers, four were found guilty of corruption and drug trafficking and were sentenced to death. The Cubans were prompt and decisive, the authors state. 'Not only because it was a problem involving ethics and principles, but also to prevent these links with the international drug market from exposing Cuba to the possibility of a US invasion. Only a few months later, in a similar situation, the United States invaded Panama under the pretext of fighting the traffic in drugs,' they explain.

He travelled alone on commercial airlines, under cover
of an assumed name and an appearance only slightly
altered by two expert touches. His briefcase contained
works of literature and numerous inhalers to relieve his
insatiable asthma; he would while away the dull hours
in hotel rooms playing endless games of chess with
himself ... Che Guevara remained in the Congo from
April to December 1965, not only training guerrillas but
leading them into battle and fighting by their side ....
After Moises Tshombe was overthrown, the Congolese
asked the Cubans to withdraw in order to facilitate
the signing of the armistice. Che left as he had come:
without fanfare.[*]

Cubans have always understood the range of Guevara's
brilliance and gumption, and scholars around the world
are now gradually opening new doors of perceptions for
those (including me) who had wrongly concluded that
we had demystified Che Guevara and his passion. Such
relatively new academic studies not only shine a light on
a rare breed of leader but also diminish systematic and
coordinated attempts by a section of Cubanologists to trash
him through unverified, sensationalist narratives.

In *Che Guevara: A Revolutionary Life* (Grove Press,
1997), Guevara's biographer Jon Lee Anderson quotes a
journalist as saying, 'If he entered a room, everything began
revolving around him . . . He was blessed with a unique
appeal . . . He had an incalculable enchantment that came

---

[*] Moises Tshombe was a puppet of the former Belgian colonists and
international mining companies

completely naturally.' Richard Gott recalls the moment in October 1963 when he first met him: 'Guevara had a charismatic attraction in real life, long before he became a Mantegna icon in death and a hypnotic image on a pop art poster in the age of Andy Warhol. Like Helen of Troy, he had an allure that people would die for.' Gott was in Bolivia, in the village of Vallegrande, four years after he first met Guevara. It was at the airfield here that Guevara's body was brought in a helicopter from La Higuera, the Bolivian village near where he was held by CIA and local operatives before being executed. Gott was one of two men (besides a Cuban-American CIA operative) who identified the body that lay with open eyes as Guevara's—because they were the only ones who had met him before. That moment perhaps changed many people's romantic ideas about an armed guerrilla revolution. It certainly did in Cuba where Fidel Castro soon began to throw his weight with greater vigour in favour of the Soviet Union and distance himself from genuine protests against the socialist empire from its constituents in Eastern Europe.

Regardless, Guevara has many more claims to fame and continued relevance than being a mere guerilla leader and a military theorist.

That day, having gorged endlessly on Guevara, I checked out the Bocoy Rum Factory, run from a typical rundown Cuban building in the Cerro neighbourhood. Not a single plaque or hoarding from the pre-revolutionary era has been removed. There are several framed photos of Che, Camilo and Fidel with cigars. This outlet is an attraction among tourists for its shop on the second floor that sells cigars, coffee, and rum—after all, Bocoy is the maker of the iconic

Legendario brand of rum. You can also buy knick-knacks here. I buy a few cigars and order their coffee. It is amazing to watch the portly middle-aged man behind the counter prepare it. He makes it the way Keralites make *adicha chaaya* (frothy tea) from a samovar by lifting the container high up and letting the hot liquid fall into the cup below. But this coffee is altogether something else—it is a bright blue liquid flame. I am sure it is tougher to make this coffee than *adicha chaaya*. The barista does it with the composure of a magician who knows his audience will be shocked by his skills. And I am. I dutifully make a video of the spectacle like a quintessential tourist.

The coffee he makes is, without doubt, the best one I have had outside of western Tamil Nadu. For a moment, I don't feel the need to have my rum cocktail at night. The flavour of coffee stays with me like a moveable feast, but I am made of sterner stuff, and there is no way I will let a Cuban evening go to waste. As the Cubans say, *Disfruta la vida!* (Enjoy life). Tonight, I will have my daiquiri until I am spiritually satiated.

Hardships of a Small Neighbour

I work hard today, visiting as many people and as many places in Havana as I can. I have to do so because I cannot stay on for long in the city, and I will soon run short of dollars and euros, my lifeline for moving around in taxis in Havana and in nearby provinces.

Classic car chauffeurs don't accept Cuban pesos or credit card payments (at least in my experience), and their rides are expensive. There are no meters, the way we have in India or elsewhere. The figure is arrived at before we start off, not always by consensus, but based on what the driver demands. In fact, I don't even try haggling the way I would in India. You see, I want no bad blood, no tension between me and the one who drives me around. I am a friend of Cuba and I love Cubans. By haggling, I don't want to bring out the worst in them. I want to bring out the best in them.

Withdrawing pesos from ATMs can be challenging because there are long queues. Even if you manage to take out pesos, they don't have much value for cab drivers whose charges are 'dollar standard'—that is the expression I use to explain to my wife when she complains about my high expenses. 'If you get a good deal with a Cuban taxi driver, half the problem is solved,' I tell her. Maybe if I had travelled in a group, I would have got a better deal per head, but I don't tell this to my wife. I am living my Cuban dream, as she had noted earlier, and some inconveniences are part of the package.

I started out with brick loads of CUP but paying for the services at Equipo de Servicios de Traductores e Intérpretes (ESTI), which supplies interpreters, and several other government offices—where you cannot pay in dollars or by credit card (in most cases)—means that I am short on local currency, too.

My state-owned hotel has no provision to use my credit card for booking a cab for me—all they do is hail a cab for you and then it is between you and the driver. They do accept credit card payments for hotel and restaurant bills, though.

On my last few days in Havana, I decide to walk around to meet people on the main thoroughfares, looking for someone who speaks English. I am lucky to run into many of them. I want to know more about what the common people, not just officials, think about their country. I manage to run into some entrepreneurs, mostly those in the hospitality segment and a few others in building-construction materials. Those in tourism-related businesses have no complaints except about one another. 'All these eateries that claim they have been around for long serve bad food. They don't care because people go anyway. We have to establish our brand and so we cannot afford to use or serve poor-quality ingredients in food,' goes the refrain.

In general, entrepreneurs in Cuba cite one big problem: lack of access to the huge American market. Like the economists I meet, they also affirm that the US sanctions are as good as international sanctions. I am asked to check out the YouTube channel 'Belly of the Beast Cuba' to know more about the problems entrepreneurs—essentially Mipymes—face in Cuba because of the stifling blockade.

One of the 'Belly of the Beast Cuba' videos I come across is about the opportunities and challenges for entrepreneurs in the country.[1] It features software development company Guajiritios and construction firm BLS Industry and Technology.

In the video, Beatriz Franco, COO of BLS Industry and Technology, notes that her company had just sixteen workers in 2018 and now they have more than seventy. For his part, Miguel Menéndez, CTO of Guajiritios, says that they started off ten years ago when five friends came together to develop software for clients. They now have more than seventy specialists in their fold. Both these teams could incorporate their companies only two years ago thanks to new reforms and rules.

BLS Industry makes liquid bases that can be used to make paint and other products and sources raw materials exclusively from Cuba. Beatriz Franco says her companies use waste products from other industries to make this liquid base. 'We advocate for a circular economy,' she asserts.

This documentary states that a quarter of a million working-age people in Cuba are now employed in Mipymes, making it an attractive proposition for those who want to earn more and do more creative work. The salaries in these entities are significantly higher than the national average, and Mipymes are expected to account for more than 10 per cent of GDP in 2023.

Miguel Menéndez says his company does business in Chile, Panama, Russia, and so on. 'The American market is essential for us,' Menéndez says, and both executives agree that the US market offers infinite potential.

Another widely covered medium business that has done well, thanks to an overseas loan, is Oscar Fernandez's Havana-based dried fruit business named Deshidratados Habana. According to a Reuters report, all that he did was upgrade antique equipment to state-of-the-art dehydrating ovens and a packaging machine. In 2022, his company produced ten times what it did a year earlier. And from ten products, they went up to fifty.

Among the most iconic faces of the rise of MSMEs is Idania del Rio, founder and creative director of Clandestina, a Havana-based fashion label which also sells its products, ranging from t-shirts and caps to socks and 'daily' bags, online. The name Clandestina is inspired by the 1987 Cuban movie *Clandestinos*. An alumnus of Instituto Superior de Diseño Industrial (Higher Institute of Industrial Design) in Havana, Rio launched her business in 2015 along with her Spanish business partner Leire Fernández. In 2016, she was part of a group of Cuban business owners that met with US President Barack Obama during his visit to Havana in April.

The company's website says, 'We are designers and artists. We are entrepreneurs and creators. We are women, and men, and anything in between. We are LGBTQ, we are of every race, and background, and beliefs.' Pledged to the ideals of sustainable fashion, the label boasts of 99 per cent Cuban design.

Surprisingly, the US embassy in Cuba offered a business training programme late in June 2023 for aspiring entrepreneurs in Cuba. A report by the Associated Press tells the story of musicians Ana María Torres and María Carla Puga who 'co-founded a store and workshop named Ama, which has a cafeteria and employs 12 people'. [2] They were among thirty entrepreneurs the embassy selected from 500 applicants. The embassy's training featured weekly online meetings covering everything from marketing tools and brand management to basic finances and the creation of web pages.

In 2023, around seventy entrepreneurs from Cuba attended a conference in Miami to learn about how to run their business 'within the confines of the embargo'. Most private businesses in Cuba deal in furniture, apparel, food and software. The conference was steered by a former Florida congressman, Joe García, a Democrat and a Cuban-American. [3]

As of 2023, Cuba's non-private sector employs over 1.6 million people, according to an analysis by the Center for the Study of the Cuban Economy, University of Havana. [4] Cuba's economy minister Alejandro Gil disclosed in July 2023 that these businesses imported $264 million and exported $6.3 million worth of goods in the first six months of 2023.

Goodwill gestures to encourage entrepreneurs in Cuba are welcome, but they appear superficial when there is great reluctance on the part of the democratic government in Washington D.C. not to lift sanctions. As Cabañas said, Obama himself never lifted the sanctions, but only re-established relations and never took the matter to the Congress.

Several American policymakers, economists, artists and opinion leaders have snubbed Miami-based Cubanologists and rabid Cuba haters to state that it is high time that the

US lifted its embargo not only because it has proved to be ineffective but also accentuated the Cuban people's hardship.

Sample this irony. The Donald Trump-run Trump Organization in 2008 sought to secure trademarks in Cuba despite President Trump saying about a decade earlier that he would not pursue business there unless the country made democratic reforms.[5] The trademark was approved two years later.[6] Though Trump never opened any locations or pursued any business on the island, his application listed a variety of commercial activities, including investing in real estate, hotels, beauty contests, casinos and golf courses. All that changed when he decided to run for President and to win elections in the swing state of Florida. Later, he became a friend of Marco Antonio Rubio whose politics is simply the politics of selling hatred against Cuba.

Sample another: There is a strange rule that the US Office of Foreign Assets Control (OFAC) imposes on ships carrying goods to any port in Cuba that restricts them from entering any port in the US for 180 days. So, if any international shipping company wishes to trade in goods or services from a Cuban port, the ship cannot dock in the US for the next six months. This restriction is applied even if a vessel has stopped in Cuba solely to purchase services such as planned ship maintenance. It sounds unbelievable, but it is true, and results, among other difficulties, in shortage of medicines and medical equipment.

And there's a second statutory restriction, the goods/passengers-on-board rule, which prohibits any vessel carrying goods or passengers to or from Cuba, or carrying goods in which Cuba or a Cuban national has an interest, from entering a US port with such goods or passengers on board, unless authorized or exempt according to OFAC.

At Cuba's tourism ministry (Ministerio de Turismo de Cuba, or MINTUR) Gihana Galindo Enríquez, commercial head, and Suyen Rivero Martínez, head of business, have closely watched tourist inflow and how US sanctions (they use the term blockade) are hurting the country's tourism. In the 1990s, there were efforts to target hotels for bomb attacks to scare potential travellers. Lately, Americans have been using more sophisticated methods such as laws and embargoes rather than direct attacks.

Just when it seemed that relations between the two countries were getting better from 2016 to 2019 (Cuba reached a record of 47,32,280 tourists in 2018, according to MINTUR), the Covid-19 pandemic and the closure of various source markets worldwide halted tourist activity. The reopening in November 2020 made it possible to present a renewed product to operators who trust in Cuba's values and attractions, these officials say. Since then, the flow of visitors has been gradually recovering with the aim of reaching pre-pandemic levels, despite the current economic conditions, they add.

Following Trump's reversal of normalization of relations with Cuba for domestic political reasons, US citizens are prohibited from engaging in tourist activities in Cuba. Only twelve limited categories are allowed to travel to Cuba, which includes business and other official trips. Worse, citizens of countries that are eligible for Electronic System for Travel Authorization (ESTA) in the US—those who do not need a regular visa to travel to the US—must apply and obtain a regular US visa if they have ever travelled to Cuba at any time in the past, effectively penalizing whoever travels to the Caribbean nation from such countries. Many European countries have released advisories on this subject—which is equivalent to a warning against travelling to Cuba.

As of 2023, Cuba's tourism sector employs 1,09,070 people. MINTUR officials I spoke to are of the view that the economic, commercial and financial blockade by the US affects all sectors of the Cuban economy, with the primary objective of 'suffocating the Cuban people'. 'The tourism sector is not exempt from this situation and has been negatively impacted, affecting services, logistics operations, and supply chain management, all of which are crucial for the tourism sector. Despite these challenges, there are other elements related to tourism that the blockade has not been able to erase, such as the warmth and hospitality of the Cuban people,' they said in a statement, adding, 'if the blockade did not exist, Cuba would be a natural market for the US and would compete on equal terms with markets such as the Dominican Republic and Mexico'.

Historically, five of the top ten countries that send tourists to Cuba are from Western Europe (Germany, Spain, France, the United Kingdom and Italy). These nations represent 15 per cent of the total volume of visitors to Cuba, MINTUR officials confirm. They believe that the decrease in arrivals from European markets lately is because of the inclusion of Cuba by the US on the list of countries that promote terrorism.

Again, MINTUR officials aver in an official response to my questions, 'Foreign banks are sanctioned when establishing relations with our country, some of them located in European countries. This has led to the complete closure of operations as a result of actions related to measures issued by the US government, particularly by the Office of Foreign Assets Control (OFAC), an intelligence and compliance agency of the US Department of the Treasury.' The US is the natural market for tourism to Cuba—and, in fact, is the second largest source of international tourism in the world.

The Cuban officials also talked about improvement in tourism infrastructure where a lot of work is in order. According to the tourism ministry, 'To reactivate Cuba's tourism infrastructure, efforts are focused in two main directions: the rescue and modernization of existing facilities that require major remodelling or restoration, and the construction of new infrastructures that are necessary for the operation of the sector.' Based on the National Development Plan until 2030, the corresponding investments are included in the annual plans of national companies, the ministry says. 'For large projects and new investments, foreign investment is also considered. Currently, the main challenges are related to transportation and road infrastructure, electrical and plumbing networks, as well as information and communication technologies,' the statement from the ministry adds.

Interestingly, American businessmen and journalists who do visit Cuba—which their country doesn't want them to visit—see a vastly different Cuba compared with what they had expected. Antonio R. Zamora, whose book I have referred to earlier, *What I Learned About Cuba By Going to Cuba*, is in favour of strengthening ties between the two countries. He is no longer the vehement opponent of Cuba that he once was, and has travelled to Cuba forty or more times since 1995 in search of rediscovering and unlearning his preconceived notions about his place of birth. 'Folks here (in the US) have no clue. They continue to see Cuba from Miami or New York or wherever they are located. You have to spend time there and talk to the Cuban people,' says this Miami-based foreign investment lawyer.[7] Kei Pritsker, a reporter with the independent media outlet *BreakThrough News*, travelled to the Caribbean country in 2022 and realized that people weren't starving to death there, nor were there police officers on every corner watching over them. He became convinced that the US slanders the country. Pritsker argues that the negative campaign is essentially due to 'history'—of how this neo-colony of the US and the playground of its corporations and the mafia changed after the Cuban Revolution, which placed the local Cuban's interests above those of corporations and gangsters from the US.[8]

How Havana used to be under the mafia (many of whom stayed in the Nacional Hotel and often chose Suite 211—the room is now called 'Mafia'—because it had a large balcony with access to the whole of the second floor) is narrated by Enrique Cirules in his book *The Mafia in Havana*, 'In 1957, the cabaret hosts stage all kinds of fantasies to entice the thousands of US tourists. The latter came to drink and dance, to test their nerve in the casinos, use cocaine, indulge themselves sexually, or satisfy any other desire or preference, however unusual. With the arrival of the moneyed crowd, the taxi drivers and profiteers began to line up; and a legion of assistants, prostitutes in fine clothing and high-class beggars emerged.'

Revolution put an end to the revelries—where nothing was sinful enough to be prohibited—and ushered in an era of bitterness. But, by 2016, the world thought US-Cuba hostilities were over or would soon be a thing of the past. Nobody perhaps captured the mood back then with greater panache than writer Richard L. Dewey did for *Rolling Stone* magazine:

> In the recent series of monumental arrivals in Cuba — Netflix, Airbnb, a US president — none looms as large as the Rolling Stones, who played to an estimated 500,000 Cubans in Havana on Friday. On an island overlooked by time for more than a half-century, the group became the focal point of life for at least a day. The iconic tongue logo sprouted up on T-shirts across Havana, and cabbies, bartenders and friendly locals asked almost anyone, 'Do you know the Rolling Stones will play tonight?' as if to confirm that the concert was indeed real.[9]

The report states that the admission for this March 2016 concert was free and that The Stones kicked off the night with the staple 'Jumpin' Jack Flash'. It was their first appearance in Havana in their 50-year career. The crowd—mostly flying Cuban flags, though Mexican, Argentinean and the Union Jack made appearances as well—gave an appreciative cheer when Jagger greeted them in Spanish, according to the report.

The euphoria didn't last long.

In a May 2023 interview with 'Belly of The Beast Cuba', US Congressman James Patrick McGovern, who has been a member of the United States House of Representatives since 1997, said that the US policy towards Cuba is an embarrassment and a miserable failure.[10] He told the interviewer that he had personally asked President Joe Biden and Secretary of State Antony Blinken to lift Cuba's designation as a state sponsor of terrorism which he said was 'just political'. He went on to call the embargo on Cuba a 'double standard given the US's extensive trade ties with other communist countries like China and Vietnam, as well as those with human-rights abuses like Egypt and Saudi Arabia'.

On his 2024 visit to Cuba, noted American scholar Jeffrey Sachs found the economic situation in the island nation to be 'extremely difficult'. In a post-tour interview with 'Belly of the Beast Cuba', he said, 'The implications of the blockade are very serious.' According to this American economist and professor at Columbia University, Cuba's income per person is now a third or fourth of what it would have been without the blockade. He expressed his deep displeasure at Donald Trump designating Cuba a state sponsor of terrorism just prior to leaving office in early 2021, a step that is seen as the major cause for a severe economic crisis and concomitant shortages. Cuba has been on that list since 1982 in the height of Reaganism until the Obama Administration in April 2015 waived it. The pressure of the sanctions is huge now that the country is back on the list.

The law is stupid, points out Sachs, adding that 'Biden is a coward' and therefore didn't reverse Trump's executive order on Cuba. As far as maintaining the social services, the Cuban government has done a good job, he avers. 'The Cuban government has been resilient but there are limits to what the government can do on its own.'

The saddest part is that although the Democrats did not need the Florida vote to win, Joe Biden surprisingly continued with Trump's aggressive Cuba policy, encouraged perhaps by the possibility of a regime change, or at least signs of a major overhaul, thanks to the July 2021 protests in the Caribbean nation. The protests started in the San Antonio de los Baños outskirts of Havana, and in Matanzas, which had seen a high number of Covid-19 cases. Although the protests turned violent in many parts of the island in the face of power blackouts, medicine shortages and other grievances, the government swept into action with top-level leaders, including the president himself, reaching the spot of the agitation to talk to people. Government officials here insist that the #SOSCuba and #SOSMatanzas campaigns did not happen automatically, nor did appeals from certain celebrities, mainly those from Miami calling for 'humanitarian intervention'. They didn't see the protests to be an outcome of an 'innocent campaign'. Though the protest was contained within hours, it continued to be reported in Miami media for over a week. There were even stories that claimed Cuban protesters were being tortured and their eyes being gouged out, killed, and so on—all without any verification and as though facts didn't matter. A month after the July 2021 protests, Aviva Chomsky penned her thoughts about a predictable and recurring trend in the Western media to denounce the 'Left' over whatever happens in Cuba. Chomsky, a professor of history and coordinator of Latin American Studies at Salem State University in Massachusetts, US, who is the author of *A History of the Cuban Revolution*, wrote in the NACLA Report on the Americas, 'Protests against scarcity, structural violence, police brutality, and corruption erupted everywhere from the United States to Colombia, Haiti, Brazil, Guatemala, Ecuador, Chile, and Argentina, just to mention a few. Those in Latin America rarely merited notice in the US news media—until they happened in Cuba.'[11] Speaking up for leftist intellectuals and activists who often come under attack in American media, Chomsky concluded in her essay, 'While we oppose the Cuban government's crackdown on the protesters, we also believe that the Cuban government's paranoia that sees the malevolent hand of the United States in every challenge to its policies is not really that far-fetched.' That the US has a reputation for sheltering, arming and financing anti-Cuba militants has been public knowledge since the time of the Revolution, especially after the Bay of Pigs Invasion of 1961.

I spoke to former CIA analyst Fulton Armstrong to understand the situation better. He is currently a senior fellow at American University's Center for Latin American and Latino Studies. Armstrong served at the US Interests Section in Havana and subsequently as senior analyst at the CIA. He has also served two terms as the director for Inter-American Affairs at the National Security Council (1995–97 and 1998–99).

Armstrong has settled on the figure of $600 million for the amount the United States has spent on 'democracy promotion', a euphemism for regime change, in Cuba over the past twenty-eight years. He tells me in an interview that under Section 109 of the 'Cuba Liberty Act'—which is almost universally called the Helms-Burton Act—the

United States has spent varying amounts of money since 1996 under the general rubric of 'democracy promotion'. He adds, 'Some administrations and most analysts have identified the sort of activities funded under that rubric as being intended to accelerate regime change on the island. The George W. Bush and Dick Cheney administration (2001–2009) straight-out referred to them as regime-change programmes. The dollar figures have varied over the years but have rarely, if ever, gone under $20 million a year. They have at times reached $40 million and $45 million a year.' The government plays shell games with the money, so a concrete chart is not available, but it is fair and entirely defensible to say that the average has been at least $25 million per year over the past 28 years, Armstrong points out. He adds, 'That makes me comfortable with my estimate of at least $600 million. I started using it when I worked on the staff of the US Senate Foreign Relations Committee, and no one in any administration has challenged it.'

He has famously stated that the 11 July 2021, protests, 'while rooted in authentic demands', were 'well-planned' with US support. He elaborates in the interview that all the information he has seen, which he has corroborated with multiple sources on the island, indicates that the protests were rooted in authentic demands. 'Cubans in Santiago (and practically everywhere on the island) face shortages of practically everything—and they did in July 2021. The evidence that the July 2021 protests were well-planned is quite easy to see, mostly in the prior coordination of the digital dissemination of information inside Cuba, which was extensively aided by external tools, particularly off-shore bots,' he emphasizes.

He goes on: 'The evidence of who controlled those bots and who funded those groups and their activities is based on sensitive sources, but I think even the circumstantial evidence is abundant enough and detailed enough to support the judgement that on-island persons—particularly the small-town activists who provided the original spark—would themselves never have the capability to run the broad-array operations that supported the protests and sustained them with video, press, etc., for so many days.'

As with all clandestine and covert operations, the persons running them put extensive resources into denying analysts, journalists and scholars the information they need to understand who is doing what, he says. These, he says, are extremely well-funded programmes that have been underway for many years. 'But what you can see on the surface should be enough to support that someone is doing something quite extensive underneath the surface. The irony is, of course, that one of the goals of the regime-change programmes is to empower people to demand transparency of government programmes, but we have no transparency on these,' Armstrong tells me.

More importantly, one must not forget the long history of anti-Cuba legislation in the US like the Torricelli Act, which was passed in 1992 by President George Bush Senior ahead of a presidential election. The same year, Bush had pardoned Orlando Bosch, the man charged with killing seventy-three people by bombing a Cuban civilian aircraft. There has been an avalanche of such acts since then, starting in 1996 with the Cuban Liberty and Democratic Solidarity (Libertad) Act, widely known as the Helms-Burton Act—a federal law designed to prevent foreign countries from engaging in international trade with Cuba by subjecting foreign nationals to travel restrictions and financial liabilities in the United States. Trump introduced more such laws, and Biden did nothing about it. Again, American sanctions are often extraterritorial in that they punish other countries who do business with Cuba by restricting them from doing business with the US. They aim to make sure that doing any transactions with Cuba comes with more risks than rewards. A six-part documentary presented by Liz Oliva Fernández and produced by Danny Glover and Oliver Stone titled *War on Cuba* offers a penetrating account of the vicious American trade war on the island nation at a time Biden, a Democrat, has become, as some writers describe, more 'Trump than Trump himself'. Far more unfair is the boycott of Cuban sportsmen and women in the United States—such as the December 2022 ban of baseball players from the country.[12]

I have my own personal experience of the US administration's political objectives.

On my arrival back from Havana to Miami—from where I am to fly to New York and then to Toronto without exiting any airport—I am asked to 'surrender' any tobacco or liquor items bought from Cuba. I thought the law applied only to those taking them for use in the United States while my destination (although via US airports) is Canada.

The lady at the counter asks me if I am carrying tobacco or alcohol from Cuba. She asks that question in a somewhat diabolical manner, meant to extract the truth from me. 'You travelled to Cuba and didn't buy cigars or rum?' It is asked in a manner feigning warmth, but then you have been around for a while on planet

Earth to know where she is heading. I am not one to lie out of fear. As soon as I say, yes of course, I am directed to go through a labyrinthine queue to seek permission from multiple officers to reach the loading area where I have to identify my checked-in baggage that contains the 'contraband'.

The whole experience is designed to be traumatic for people not used to officers acting 'tough'. At immigration in Miami, after I declare that I am carrying all the cigars that I have written about in the previous pages of this book, I assert I am only transiting through the US, but my destination is Canada, a third country.

After a brief interview that is more like an interrogation, the officer in charge announces: 'I am going to empty your rum bottle and burn your cigars. You can see it for yourself if you want to. We won't use it.'

It is clear now that this is a meaningless law and that he is about to execute it. He lets me keep the cigar cutter that works like a miniature guillotine. They call it the guillotine cigar cutter. I feel like asking him to confiscate that as well but hold back my outrage because a US-based friend had advised against being combative with American officers: 'There is no way they will agree they are wrong. The more you argue, the meaner they become. On the other hand, if they feel you are obedient and repentant they won't harm you.' I keep silent and stay calm.

The officer then hands me a sheet of paper with the logo and name of US Customs and Border Protection. Under the subhead 'title', it says: Bringing in Cuban goods and/or cigars into the United States.

Under another subhead, 'content', the text says:

Effective 24 September 2020, authorised travellers may no longer return to the United States with alcohol and/or tobacco products acquired in Cuba as accompanied baggage for personal use.

Persons authorised to travel to Cuba may purchase alcohol and tobacco products while in Cuba for personal consumption in Cuba.

Persons subject to United States jurisdiction may purchase or acquire Cuban-origin merchandise, including alcohol and tobacco products, while in a third country for personal consumption outside the United States.

It goes on (in English and Spanish) in the same vein.

I don't watch them pour out my cherished Cuban rum into wherever they empty it or how they incinerate my fine cigars. I am filled with bitterness and scorn. In India, even the most ferocious police officers I have met have relented in the face of reason. Here, only the uniform is right.

At that very moment, I realize why Ambassador Cabañas, who knows the US administration only too well, is unenthusiastic about the prospects of the United States lifting the blockade anytime soon, no matter who resides inside the White House, a Democrat or a Republican.

My indignation devours me all through the rest of my journey to Toronto. It had taken a lot of careful research before I hand-picked those cigars for my friends. The cigars looked as though they had life. Those men, they cremated them alive. Rest in peace!

I think of the Havana Club Cuban rum, which is exported to more than 140 countries of the world except the US. That is a message in a bottle. That doesn't die. From the sugarcane plantations of nineteenth-century Santiago de Cuba to UNESCO's intangible cultural heritage list, from the Caribbean slave quarters of yore to royal palaces, from the underground shelters of Cuban national heroes who fought the Spanish in the late nineteenth century to modern luxury resorts worldwide, Cuba's light rum is a masterpiece, the most useful ingredient for the finest of cocktails. And it continues to thrive and evolve, sanctions be damned.

Crashing Waves Over the Malecon

I have a dream about the Malecon. From my room in the Nacional de Cuba Hotel, I begin to roll involuntarily through the corridor, onto the lift, the lobby and the lawn, to reach the marine drive they call Malecon. There is a saying in Havana that the Malecon is the sofa of the Cuban people. They come here to enjoy the ocean, sit back and relax, watch people, date, fish and occasionally swim if the sea isn't rough.

In my dream, I roll down, without being seen by the hotel staff or the forever alert bartenders in the bar along the left side of the lawn or the enthusiastic waiters at the restaurant on the right that serves heavenly Cuban food. Neither the performing musicians nor the guests in the hotel roaming about or dancing away notice me roll past. The cannon that fought the empires sees me. So do the chairs and the doors and the green grass. They conspire with me and don't raise an alarm while I allow myself to fall to the road. It is a painful fall, but I am prepared for it. I jump into the sea and swim. The water is neither cold nor hot, and I enjoy floating on the mellow waves of the night.

Then I wake up.

I haven't yet recovered from that dream when I sit down with a young couple that evening at the bar lounge in my hotel. We had met earlier at an eatery and decided to meet again. My hope is that they will invite me home, but they haven't yet suggested it. I offer them the cigars I had bought from the cigar-and-rum shop at the Nacional. The boy looks at the yellow cylindrical packaging of the cigar— it is a Montecristo. He seems impressed. We sip our cocktail drinks. Mine is Cuba Libre, although I have decided it is not my favourite—I have developed a kind of disdain for cola. The man, who wears a Che beret, is as strong as a bull but has the innocent face of a baby. His poison is daiquiri. The lady has a beer.

In a while, we order a *Lechon asado a lo guajiro* (piglet roast) and *Langosta maripasa al carbon* (charcoal lobster). I am not hungry, but they are. They polish off their plates and I note the quantity of salads and vegetables they consume. They are earthy, messy eaters, like us Malayalis, but they eat more of what they don't get through the public distribution system: olives, tomatoes, leafy vegetables, cheese, dry fruit, fruit and other vegetables. They simply gorge on them, much more than they relish meat.

The boy, who is almost a man, is twenty-two and the woman is twenty-five. He is a boxer without a boxer's nose, and she is a history scholar who models once in a while and is currently training in wrestling. She has the aura of a tigress in meditation. The boy says he wanted to be the Teófilo Stevenson of New Cuba. He explains to me, as though I am hearing it for the first time, what Stevenson, one of only three boxers ever to win three Olympic gold medals, had to say when he was offered several millions of dollars to fight the legendary Muhammed Ali in the US sometime in the 1970s. While declining the offer because he would have had to relinquish his status as a Cuban amateur, Stevenson said, 'What is one million dollars compared to the love of eight million Cubans?' The boy's chest swells and his face lights up when he says it. 'Have you heard of him?' he asks. I say no, allowing him the pleasure of being the first to introduce such a legend to me. He smiles wryly: 'The world knows Americans even if they are half great, but not us Cubans.'

I console him, saying, 'All that will change soon. They know Fidel for a longer period, much more than any President of the United States, including those who tried to bump him off.' The girl agrees. She immediately brings up a book named *Executive Action: 634 Ways to Kill Fidel Castro* by the former chief of Cuban counterintelligence, Fabián Escalante. The book, she says, lists out major US covert operations to assassinate Castro. The discussion then swerves towards the connection between sports in Cuba and its gold medal haul in the Olympics—the young man says Cuba has won the maximum medals among all Latin American countries although it had not taken part in the games for several decades. 'We dominate in judo and boxing,' he says. Since 1972, boxers from Cuba have won 42 gold medals at the Olympic Games (the latest being Cuban lightweight boxer Erislandy Alvarez at the Paris 2024 Olympic Games), more than any other nation in those five decades despite the country not being part of the 1984 and 1988 Olympics events.

The boy spends a few minutes teaching me how to smoke the cigar without inhaling. I get it right the fourth time and they both cheer in delight.

'You are Cuban now,' the boy exclaims.

As a sportsman, he is not supposed to smoke. Neither should she, she states. 'But then there are no injunctions or commandments that you cannot enjoy once in a blue moon,' I offer in an idiomatic way, and they understand me only partly. 'Yes, we have some restrictions. We are asked to eat right,' says the guy.

'Are the rations enough?' I ask. I regret asking that question immediately.

'We eat enough, the bodegas are not our only source of food,' the young man says, with a hint of indignation.

The bodegas are the ration shops from where Cubans have, since the Revolution, collected rations at heavily subsidized rates, carrying with them the Libreta, a booklet in which the official marks whatever they have bought. The concept is very similar to the ration cards in India.

'Oh, I am sorry. I am being indiscreet and asking you for personal details,' I say.

'No. No problem,' says the young lady, her warmth thawing the sudden chill in the conversation. She rummages in her backpack and then offers me a fruit that looks like a mango. I later learn that it tastes like one too.

We talk about fruits in Cuba and Kerala, and how some of them are also used for making alcohol. The boy tells me his favourite is *Guayabita del Pinar* (from Pinar del Rio) produced from cane sugar and blended with *guayabita* (little guavas). After tasting, you are supposed to say something that translates to 'damn', he advises me. The expression you show is irritation, but you do it because you like it so much, he says. I love the logic. I am familiar with seasoned drinkers among the old-timers in India, especially

Kerala, who exhibit a facial expression of revulsion as soon as they consume the drink: it is not because they dislike it, but because they relish it the most. In Cuba, you say '*carajo*' (pronounced as kaaraaho) when you finish a really good drink (Like, *oh fuck!* Or, *oh shit!*).

The girl talks about her parents. She uses the word 'folks'. She says her father had been an engineer and mother a nurse and they now have a private business. 'They run a casa particular in Matanzas and they have some money. That is why I can go boating and ziplining here in Cuba and for holidays in Panama,' she says.

The boy looks around at the hotel and says, 'Most rich foreigners who come to Cuba check into luxury hotels, not into government-run ones, even if they are in excellent condition. Are you happy with your stay at the Nacional?'

'Yes. I am,' I say truthfully. 'There is a lot of history. I like the ambience. They say it was there that Graham Greene wrote parts of his pre-revolutionary book *Our Man in Havana,* which pokes fun at espionage work.'

Neither of them has any opinion on the book. They ask me a few questions about India. I blurt out the usual answers like, 'You know democracy has its drawbacks, but then that is the beauty of it too.'

We talk about Coppelia (an ice cream parlour chain in Cuba), the 1994 movie *Strawberry and Chocolate,* which was shot in Cuba (its set is now part of the famous eatery La Guarida), and rumba dance. The girl, who has been silent for a while, regains her enthusiasm and switches to a new subject: coffee. She informs me about the BioCubaCafe project—which I learn later is a collaboration between Cuba and the Agroforestry Business Group and the Lavazza

Group, both from Italy, with the cooperation of the Agency for Cultural and Economic Exchange—to make and sell Cuban coffee produced without chemical components. It is done by over 170 coffee growers from nine municipalities in eastern Cuba. I make a mental note to buy a packet of Cuban coffee for my wife.

It's time to say goodbye. I walk them to the entrance of the hotel and then—because I am curious to see their *riquimbili*—I walk a short distance along with them to where they have parked it, hidden in a small alley. Riquimbilis (pronounced 'rick-in-billy') are improvised motorcycles. Once again, this is the *resolver* concept at work, or what we call jugaad in India. A chain-saw motor is attached to a regular old bicycle, along with a plastic bottle or some other container for the fuel tank, and a bent pipe for the exhaust. The result is noisy, but it gets you around. Though riquimbilis are illegal, the young couple tells me the authorities often look away.

I go back into my room and slip into a rum-induced sound sleep. I wake at dawn and go for a walk. The grass has the scent of draft beer. A lady in a blue shirt and trousers stands watching the vast ocean looking like Picasso's *Garçon à la Pipe*. The Malecon is leisurely lying in wait to get baked soon by the sun, now vermillion and mild. The wind blows like a migratory bird on a fantastic voyage. Peacocks honk. Two or three hens on the hotel lawn cluck their way to a puddle. Then there is a business-as-usual sound of glasses falling and breaking into pieces from somewhere inside the hotel. Motorists are just beginning to hit the roads.

Savouring the lingering taste of Cuban coffee inside my mouth, I head towards the edge of the lawn to inspect whether it is possible to fall off from there, as I did in my dream, and live to tell the tale. I sit there on a bench, open my YouTube app on the phone and play *The Lonely Shepherd* by Gheorghe Zamfir, the Romanian master of the pan flute, to snap out of a sudden sense of desolation. The music works faster than an SOS pill for panic attacks.

Resistance and Transition

Cuba is unique in more ways than one. The country has been under the longest trade embargo in modern history—since 1960. Since the Revolution, the US has seen thirteen presidents remit office. All these American presidents have remitted office after failing to achieve regime change in the Caribbean country through what the Cubans consider as the economic asphyxiation of their homeland.

Christopher Columbus first reached the Bahamas in the year 1492 before heading to Cuba, which was the first geographical entity in that part of the world that attracted his attention. He is believed to have said of Cuba, 'The most beautiful island that eyes ever beheld.' Columbus never travelled to any part of what is now called the United States. The Italian explorer, who launched voyages sponsored by the Spanish monarchy, was on his way to the east along with his crew and they thought they had reached the shores of India.

For centuries, after Columbus and his men returned to Spain from the Caribbean in early 1493, Cuba endured the Spanish conquest and the near extinction of its indigenous races, called the Taino, because of persecution and epidemics. The Taino people introduced the concept of hammocks to the world and offered the roots of words such as barbeque, canoe, and hurricane to their colonizers.[1]

In 1511, Diego de Velázquez, who had accompanied Columbus on his second voyage in late 1493, founded the first Spanish settlement on the island and became its governor. The indigenous name for the place was Baracoa, which still exists.[2] Velázquez went on to create a total of seven urban settlements that included Santiago de Cuba and Havana in the early sixteenth century. The island also witnessed the infusion of African slaves to work in gold mines, sugar plantations and tobacco fields.[3] The Spanish managed to keep other colonial powers away, including the British who had occupied Havana after the Seven Years' War in 1762, but the British returned the city to the Spanish in exchange for Florida eleven months later.

All through the Spanish conquest, especially in the nineteenth century, the Americans had eyes on Cuba. In 1848, American President James K. Polk offered to buy the island for $100 million but the offer was rejected by Spain.

Cuba had been vulnerable to attacks from pirates and other reckless men from Europe for long until the Spanish strengthened it with forts and walls. But the locals began a decades-long struggle for independence from Spanish rule in the late 1860s. The explosion of the USS Maine in Havana harbour on 15 February 1898 was the pretext for the US to intervene in the Cuban War of Independence and to trounce the Spanish within months in what became known as the Spanish–American war. Spanish control of Cuba ended on 16 July 1898. The Americans didn't do it to help a beleaguered local population in the neighbourhood against a colonial European power, but out of neocolonial designs. They themselves annexed Cuba in 1898 and ruled till 1902, with the aim of turning Cuba into a client state. In exchange for withdrawing from Cuba and rendering it a vassal state, the US brought in what came to be known as the Platt Amendment of 1901, which stipulated seven conditions one of which was the right of the 'United States to intervene unilaterally in Cuban affairs'.

The veterans of the Cuban liberation struggle were shocked by the American behaviour. They couldn't come to terms with the Americans engaging in the transfer of power talks with the Spanish without them. These parleys were held in Paris and elsewhere and Cubans were considered by the American generals and politicians as people incapable of self-governing themselves. In place of the Cuban flag, what came up after the Spanish flag was the American one. Over the next years, Americans tried to educate Cubans to become loyal servants of the American cause, and teachers in the newly created schools were taken to the US to be brainwashed. But Cubans resisted. To cut a long story short, the four-year total occupation of Cuba by the Americans revealed their aversion to Cuban self-rule. Their politics of condescension is much older than the Cuban Revolution and Fidel Castro, or communism in the island nation.

Although the Republic of Cuba was established in 1902, Cuba remained a client state of the US with a puppet government in place. By 1907, foreigners, most of them Americans, owned an estimated 60 per cent of land in rural Cuba; the resident Spanish owned 15 per cent and only 25 per cent was in the hands of the Cubans.[4] Of the twenty most productive sugar hubs in Cuba in 1925, only one was Cuban and the rest were American. Cuba was a money-spinner, nothing else, for the Americans. Among the critics of the puppet regime, not even those who fled were safe. Cuban revolutionary Julio Antonio Mella, one of the founders of the original Communist Party of Cuba, was shot dead in Mexico City in 1929 by assailants who were allegedly linked to Gerardo Machado, then President of Cuba who was notorious for being repressive. It is a different matter that the Mexican government of the time blamed his death on internal rivalry among the communists.

The Platt Amendment continued to be in place until 1934, and after it was repealed, new laws were brought in to ensure American supremacy over the sugar markets of the country. Under America's remote-control rule, which lasted until the Cuban Revolution of 1959, dissent was quelled, and puppets were anointed and promoted in Cuba. Successive US Presidents of the time turned the island nation into a wild holiday destination for its rich and a hub for its mafia, ninety miles from the mainland. It was the equivalent of the British Raj in India, and the American corporations and gangsters made enormous profits as millions of Cubans lived in abject poverty.

Incidentally, there is something uncanny about the time between the aborted attack by Castro and his team on the Moncada Barracks in Santiago de Cuba on 26 July 1953, and the Revolution of 1 January 1959. The latter, a triumphal and epochal event, took place five years, five months, and five days after the Moncada attack. I read this interesting fact in an account of the Cuban Revolution in Malayalam in a book by the late C. Bhaskaran, a Marxist intellectual and writer.

Cubans are also inventive in their political messaging. Can you imagine that decades before the Aam Aadmi Party (AAP) in Delhi, India, came up with their election symbol of broom, Cuba already had their share of broom politics? Cuban politician Eduardo René Chibás, who founded the Orthodox Party in 1947, was vehemently opposed to the corruption rampant in Cuba and the American mafia treating the island as a haven. Not only did he extensively use radio to communicate with the people, but his supporters brandished brooms in processions to highlight his message of clean governance.

Then came the era of Fidel Castro.

After the 1953 Moncada uprising, Castro served a prison term in the Isle of Pines where, it is said, the future leader of Cuba read twelve to fourteen hours a day. He immersed himself in philosophy and fiction, mostly masterpieces like *Crime and Punishment* and *Les Miserables* and others. It was here that he also read Karl Marx's *Capital, The Eighteenth Brumaire of Louis Bonaparte, The Class Struggles in France*, and so on. He was released within two years in the face of student protests.

What Castro did best in the initial years while he was campaigning for the Revolution from the heights of the Sierra Maestra mountains along with fellow guerillas was making use of publicity to his advantage and becoming the talk of the town. He knew the importance of propaganda. While he was waiting for the right occasion to strike at the Batista regime in Cuba along with other guerilla leaders with whom he lived in the mountains from 1957, he managed to offer interviews to *The New York Times* and CBS, and in the process, grabbed the limelight once again. Reading those articles and hearing Castro speak, even the American public was awed at the charismatic, courageous and handsome young leader, who was barely thirty at the time.

The Revolution was not overtly a communist one to begin with. Most comrades of Castro were die-hard Cuban nationalists who fought for freedom and not for communism. Most of them championed the ideals of nineteenth-century Cuban nationalist, poet, and philosopher José Martí who worked to end Spanish rule in Cuba. Talking to reporters in New York in April 1959, Fidel himself said he was a man of democracy and that he was not a communist. Yet, there was a lack of clarity and debate about his political affiliation. That debate continues: was he a communist to begin with or did he become one later? Or was his political philosophy a fusion of Marx and Martí?

This ability to garner publicity was visible in New York in September 1960 when he attended a UN summit. He stormed out of the Hotel Shelburne on Lexington Avenue over their demand for a hefty deposit and headed to Hotel Theresa in the black neighbourhood of Harlem. At this spot, Castro drew crowds and met several world leaders, including then Indian Prime Minister Jawaharlal Nehru, African American icon Malcolm X, Russian leader Khrushchev and others. David Talbot writes in his best-selling *The Devil's Chessboard: Allen Dulles, the CIA, and the Rise of America's Secret Government* (William Collins, 2015):

Castro's mastery of the media game was on full display during his Harlem sojourn. After Eisenhower snubbed him by not inviting him to an official reception for Latin leaders, the Cuban premier responded by inviting Theresa's all-black staff to a steak dinner in the hotel banquet room with him and the popular Almeida. When articles suddenly began appearing in New York newspapers, alleging that the Theresa was overrun with hookers, Fidel again parried the propaganda thrust, declaring in his speech at the UN, 'They began spreading the news all over the world that the Cuban delegation had lodged in a brothel. For some, a humble hotel in Harlem, a hotel inhabited by Negroes of the United States, must obviously be a brothel.'

The hotel is defunct now, though the 13-storey building still stands and is designated as a New York City landmark. While in NYC, I visited the spot in Harlem and found myself sharing an evocative moment with some fellow Malayali friends who came along.

In the early years of independence, there wasn't a visible push towards communism except from Raul Castro and Che Guevara. The Cuban leadership veered towards the Soviets after learning of how the Americans were training Cuban expats and arming rebels within to wage a war against Fidel Castro. After receiving intelligence about CIA-sponsored coup attempts against him, Castro openly turned to the Soviet Union for help and soon there were nuclear missiles facing the US in its own backyard. The Cold War heightened and pushed the world to the brink of a nuclear war, but restraint on the part of John F. Kennedy and Nikita Khrushchev, the leaders of the US and USSR, respectively, prevented a dangerous conflagration. The USSR withdrew its missiles from Cuba and the US from Turkey, where the Americans had placed similar missiles. Castro was miffed at being kept in the dark about the negotiations between the US and the USSR, but Moscow would soon find ways to placate him. Importantly, a world war was averted, but Cuba was punished with trade embargoes. To date, they are still in place.

The aim of all American presidents since Dwight D. Eisenhower has been to get the people who elected Castro to power to throw him out—it never happened. He died in November 2016 and had been in retirement since 2008 when his brother Raul assumed power. Raul served as the first secretary of the Communist Party of Cuba from 2011 to 2021 and as President of Cuba from 2008 to 2018. Miguel Mario Díaz-Canel, an engineer with a PhD in technical sciences, stepped into Raul Castro's shoes, occupying both the key positions he had held. Despite prophecies of the communist party's fall from grace, it is still firmly in the saddle.

But the experiment in America's backyard with socialism has not been easy, especially since the fall of the Soviet Union in 1991. Soviet ships had supplied Cuba with the necessary oil, machinery and various other commodities, and Cuba dispatched sugar, cigars, nickel and so on in return. The fall of the Soviet Bloc in 1989–90 and then the Soviet Union itself a little while later was a huge blow. But Cuba has survived the vagaries of time and sanctions for more years without Soviet support than with it. The Russian embassy tower is still a landmark building on Quinta Avenida (Fifth Avenue) in Miramar, but its magnificence has obviously faded, and it looks like a pale shadow of what it once was, when it brimmed with Soviet officials and agents.

Interestingly, Cubans achieved several feats without Soviet supervision even when the latter was still a superpower. Notably, among its international interventions to ensure that leftist forces prevailed in other countries, Cuba's presence in Angola was instrumental in stopping the South African army from assailing the People's Movement for the Liberation of Angola (MPLA), which had led the liberation struggle against the Portuguese. Cubans assisted the MPLA against the South African army, which eventually withdrew and stopped aiding MPLA's rivals in Angola. Cubans did it with local help and without much Soviet assistance. The Cubans were in Angola from 1975 until 1991 when South Africa was an apartheid state backed by the US. 'Cuba withdrew from Angola with honour, and it could rightfully share in the credit for Namibia's independence,' conceded Major Jayson N. Williams of the United States Army.[5] Marquez pointed out that Angola finally gave the Cubans the satisfaction of the great victory that they so badly needed. The Americans soon—especially after the Battle of Cuito Cuanavale in Angola in 1988—forced South Africa to the negotiating table.[*] Nelson Mandela recalled later, praising Castro, 'The decisive defeat of the aggressive apartheid forces [in Angola] destroyed the myth of the invincibility of the white oppressor.'[6] Alongside, with the Soviet empire crumbling, the US's interest in fighting

---

[*] The South African newspaper *Weekly Mail* described it as 'a crushing humiliation' for apartheid South Africa. The publication reported on 1 July 1988, 'Africa's strongest army is without certain air superiority in a war which more resembles the trenches of the Somme than more familiar counterinsurgency war of modern times.' It was the biggest war fought in Africa post-World War II.

wars where their archenemy was not actively involved began to wane.

Now, decades later, allowing an experiment with socialism in Latin America to flourish and succeed is not in American interest and its policies are proof of its convictions. Notwithstanding global condemnations that we have discussed before, the US has refused to budge, often finding support from Israel alone.

The blockade has led to disenchantment among residents who were once votaries of a socialist Cuba. A chunk of them, meanwhile, aren't overly enthused about the ongoing privatization either, especially outside of cities. Many Cubans appear confused and say that all they want are steady supplies—of essential food items, including milk, medicines, cell phones and batteries. On the streets, people mostly appear perturbed or anxious, and, if they are in long queues outside meat stores or other rationing facilities, they stand bored and irritated. The agony of not having much to choose from upsets ordinary people, especially because they are now exposed through social media, friends, family and occasional travel to sprawling malls and the consumerist culture of advanced countries where people earn, they assume, enough to enjoy the varieties of life.

Cooked meals are available at affordable rates in government-run cafeterias, but then one must put up with the monotony of eating similar kinds of food every day. A thirty-two-year-old woman in Old Havana, who looks much older than her age, remarks, 'The quality is not good, and I would say it's not much food either.' She rues that the long lines for buying groceries or medicines also include older people. 'The government sort of assigns social workers to senior citizens and those who live in the poorest conditions, but I cannot tell you how well they fulfil this purpose. Sometimes, people in the community help them. I would say this all depends on people's kindness,' she explains.

One person, a middle-aged man with three generations living in his household, tells me, 'Pensioners have the lowest income in the country. It's only 1500 pesos, unless they worked for the armed forces (Fuerzas Armadas Revolucionarias, or FAR, in Spanish). People who work there have many, many benefits, and depending on their ranks, their salaries are higher, and therefore pensions are higher.'

He shares his experience of the ration shops, which distribute subsidized items, 'We only get five eggs per person a month. Sometimes in Havana we are lucky and get seven, but not in other provinces.' He says that if he were to depend on government stores alone for foodstuff, he would end up spending around five months at a time without coffee. 'I think it's being distributed with greater frequency in some areas of the city. And Cubans love coffee, so,' he shrugs, his unfinished sentence expressing both resignation and longing.

A young undergraduate student from the university enlightens me with more details about the long queues for essentials, especially after Covid-19. 'There are basic products that you can buy in these CUP stores and lately there is a shortage of things so there is a cap on how much one household can buy. It's ten pounds of chicken, one package of sausage, one litre of cooking oil, two packages of minced meat, and one kilo of laundry detergent. If you are lucky, you can buy them all on the same day. If not, you'll have to go to the store to see when they start distributing the missing product,' she explains, adding that these quantities are for an entire family, regardless of the number of members they have. 'For me, because I live alone,' she says, 'this would be enough for a whole month. Perhaps it will also be enough for a household of three people if they plan their meals well. But for more than four people, it's not enough. And they would have to go to the informal market or the private sector to buy the rest of the products,' she emphasizes, standing outside Havana University, the alma mater of the likes of Castro and hundreds of other revolutionaries whose names have been lost to history. It was here that the country's student movement played a pivotal political role in the 1950s, including the violent calls to free Castro and his comrades from jail following the Moncada attack.

All shortages are not caused directly by the blockade, but by supply-chain constraints indirectly linked to the sanctions. For instance, Cuba gets its milk powder from New Zealand, but since the country is often short of cash, there are concomitant delays.

But what American reporters and TV crews, who visit Cuba to voyeuristically portray its poverty and shortage of essential goods, do not acknowledge is the freedom they have in Cuba. Surveillance of journalistic activities by foreigners is almost non-existent. Though independent local journalists do complain of interference by the state and of being forced to go into exile in the face of harassment,[7] there are no reports yet of any journalist in Cuba losing their life over their work, unlike in other Latin American countries, or even India. Fidel Castro told Barbara Walters in his 1977 interview that the Cuban idea of freedom of the press isn't the same as the one in the US—and that criticism of socialism is not welcome in local media.[8] But this appears to be a theoretical concept. For all practical reasons, at present, there is no curtailment of freedom for foreign TV crews and bloggers landing in Cuba and broadcasting its poverty and food shortages to the world.

Ironically, what doesn't come under intense scrutiny in the Western media or in most blogs—apart from routine reporting of press conferences and briefings by White House officials, including the President—is the American obsession with prolonging its criminal and inhuman sanctions against Cuba, a country that has multiple strengths across a variety of fields, including biotechnology and pharmaceuticals.

Let's not forget that propaganda from the US demonizing Cuba as a terrorist state is not Trump's doing either. It is much, much older. As early as 1978, John Stockwell, a former officer of the Central Intelligence Agency (CIA) and chief of its Angola Task Force chief, had spilled the beans about the spy agency's propaganda against the Third World, especially Cuba, in his tell-all book *In Search of Enemies: A CIA Story*. He had also given interviews since the late 1970s, calling out the CIA for unleashing lies to trash Cuba. Essentially, all such misinformation campaigns are an outcome of a tragedy of errors on the part of administrations that chose to ally with vote banks and refused to make healthy foreign-policy decisions. For his part, Zamora says in his book on Cuba that Kennedy is always blamed for the Bay of Pigs setback for the US, although it was the previous D.

Eisenhower Administration that 'allowed Cuba to develop a massive purchase programme in 1959, two years before the invasion'.[9] It was impossible even for the US to take on a country that had acquired weapons and trained its troops well. Many of these weapons came from the US's allies.

Later, what Castro said in an interview with Robert MacNeil of PBS NewsHour in 1985 confirmed the cause of the military transition of Cuba at that time: necessity.[10] The Cuban leader said in the TV chat that, thanks to the Bay of Pigs Attack of 1961, Cuba began to fear more such attacks and so it aligned with the Soviet Union and installed missiles in Cuba. The Cuban leader also said it was an outcome of America's actions, not his or the Soviet Union's.

Meanwhile, Zamora also points out that the Americans don't take into consideration how Cuba has changed from its early decades to the 1990s, after the decline of the Soviet Union. Cuba adopted a new Constitution in 1992 transforming into a secular state from the atheist state it was earlier. It also allowed for private ownership in real estate in certain cases and brought in a new foreign investment code. When Pope John Paul II visited Cuba in 1998, it was an ideal moment for the Americans to build bridges, but they continued to remain sceptical and indifferent. The Pope said, 'Cuba should be opened to the world and the world should be opened to Cuba.'[11] American reluctance to change was conspicuous until Obama made the right noises starting in 2013. And then, when the world thought Americans were fully prepared to bury the hatchet, Trump came to power and put things in reverse gear.

Strikingly, when you fly down to Havana from the US on a Delta Air flight, the airline brings along American cleaning staff—even if it wastes seats and costs money—presumably because they don't want Cubans to do the job. It makes great sense in this context to quote Wayne S. Smith, former US diplomat and author who has written books on US-Cuba relations, 'Cuba has the same effect on US administrations as the full moon has on wolves: it is an obsession.' The blockade has escalated to become the most complex, prolonged and inhuman act of economic warfare ever committed against any nation. As mentioned earlier, Cubans estimate the losses accumulated during this time at more than $144,413,400,000 (more than $144 billion) at current prices as of 2022. Since the sanctions are conceived to impede trading relations with third countries, it has hurt foreign investment and literally cut off most sources of revenue for Cuba, which is seeking its rightful place and dignity in a world dominated by the US.

Like most segments, the education sector too feels the pinch of embargoes. According to the Cuban foreign ministry, the damage caused by the blockade to the educational sector from March 2022 to February 2023 is higher than $75 million. It states that students cannot access more than 300 websites that are of interest to computer scientists since they are blocked for Cuban IP addresses. Such a policy that wickedly fuses malice and schadenfreude and is deplored by the world has no moral justification or legitimacy.

There is easily a lot of scope for improvement of relations between the two countries. Voting preferences could change, altering political compulsions. The Cuban-American diaspora is not a monolithic entity that is staunchly opposed to the loosening of sanctions on Cuba. On the other hand, a visit to Cuba proves that Cuban

Americans are at the forefront of making the most of the changes sweeping modern Cuba, which is blessed with natural resources that include cobalt, nickel, iron ore, copper, salt, silica, manganese, timber and petroleum besides gold. It is home to the third-highest reserves of what is often called the precious metal of the future, cobalt, after the Democratic Republic of Congo and Australia. Cobalt offers Cuba great promise because the precious metal is used for lucrative business purposes, including making batteries for smartphones, tablets, laptops and electric vehicles. Cobalt is particularly abundant in the Moa region, in the east of the island. The lack of adequate foreign investment hurts mining and deprives the country of related economic gains, but the potential for growth remains. Italian geopolitical analyst and author Emanuel Pietrobon has stated that Western countries, including the United States, are deficient in nickel and cobalt, which means that a Russian-BRICS-Cuban cooperation in the sector could considerably increase their negotiating power with Washington.[12] He is of the view that Cuba is a country with enormous significance in the world scene because it is one country that makes the Americans lose sleep. 'Cuba has a role to play in the current hegemonic struggle between the West and the Rest. Russia and the BRICS should take advantage of its geostrategic and geopolitical position and act accordingly (to help Cuba tide over its current difficulties)—Cuba's salvation might mean the multipolar transition's culmination,' he says.

Cuba is also a natural habitat for hundreds of thousands of species of flora and fauna. The bright side of the sanctions has been that in and around Cuba, in the ocean and in cenotes, many species of fish and animals that had gone extinct elsewhere in the Caribbean— due to industrialization—have survived here. But then, the challenge of preserving them and monetizing such attractions remains an arduous task. Trafficking in rare species, along with increased tourist footfall, poses a grave threat to Cuba's virgin forests and sea life.

Now, let's look at what the Cuban Revolution has done for the people. Zamora says in his book that the Agrarian Reforms Law of 17 May 1959 gave ownership of land to more than 1,00,000 small peasants and their families, benefitting more than 5,00,000 people. The Urban Reform Law of 17 October 1960, according to his studies, allowed tenants to buy a house over twenty years with a payment of close to 30 per cent of their monthly income. The Revolution also ensured greater participation of women in the country's workforce and government. Indeed, women played a crucial role in the years leading to the 1959 triumph, with Cuban revolutionaries such as Melba Hernández, Celia Sánchez, Haydée Santamaría and Vilma Espín being some of them. The literacy programme was a huge hit too. While upper-class Cubans migrated abroad, those in the middle and lower classes stood to benefit from the Cuban government's policies in the initial decades. True, aspiring classes are now looking for an end to their hardship, but the 2021 policies have given a section of them a sense of hope amidst all the shortage, endless queues and daily frustrations of long waits for transport. Even so, continued American sanctions are hurting the Cubans, forcing many young people to sell their properties and whatever they own and move abroad to start struggling anew in pursuit of their ambitions.

It would be wise therefore on the part of the US to stop using its Cuba policy as a mere electoral ploy, which amounts to making a great power appear abysmally petty, like a selfish Big Brother with wounded pride and an overbearing ego. Instead, the White House could act maturely and admit that it failed to assassinate Castro, at least since he is now dead, and to topple Cuban socialism— or socialism with Cuban characteristics—and instead become a force multiplier of the new trends buffeting the Caribbean nation, a tourist paradise known for three Ss (sun, sand and salsa), three Rs (rum, rumba and romance) and three Cs (cigars, classic cars and communism).

As I leave Havana, I wait outside the José Martí International Airport to look at the vast expanse of green outside, and the pregnant white clouds against the tranquil blue skies. The resplendence is familiar. This and all the other sights I have seen in Cuba are as vivid as the photos and descriptions that had mesmerized me in my teens. I am overcome by an intense sense of déjà vu. As a Malayali fed on books about the heroism of the Cuban Revolution, this visit was like a destiny waiting to be fulfilled. I ended up learning, unlearning and relearning. I had amazing access and exposure to a world I had so far read about and watched from across the seas. It is a nation in economic turmoil largely thanks to the blockade. Although the spirit of the Revolution is alive in the minds of the older generation, the younger lot do not want to know the reasons why they are suffering, and instead they want results. Which explains the exodus of the young.

The highlight of all was the connect I could establish with Cuban art and culture. Certain names linger in my thoughts—the names of singers, movies and filmmakers who throw open the portals to understanding Cuba. I tend to associate them with the mystic spelling of a perfect morning coffee: musicians Bole de Nieve, Teté Caturla, Ibrahim Ferrer, movies such as *La Última Cena* (The Last Supper), *El Cuerno de la Abundancia* (Horn of Plenty), *Lista de Espera* (Waiting List) and so on. The influence of the great Cuban writer Alejo Carpentier cannot be underrated either, and the sublime voice of Osdalgia left me craving for more.

It occurs to me that this defiant island nation has many lessons to offer. It is a country that shoulders endless burdens. Cubans are still trying to find the meaning of the absurdity of the decades-old US blockade and so is the rest of the world. The Americans have dramatically changed their policies for others, but not for Cuba. Since 1995, the United States has been friends with its one-time nemesis, Vietnam, a country that humiliated them, trounced them, and punctured their inflated ego. But Cuba—which is struggling to find new friends to tide over its economic woes and has since March 2024 famously re-established diplomatic ties with South Korea after sixty-five years, its ally North Korea's arch-rival—is still an outcast for the Americans who seem persistent on clashing with it long after the Cold War is over. It is as though the Americans and the Cubans are like blood brothers vying to see who will blink first. As much as the situation can be put down to American condescension and farcical errors, a sense of tragedy bestrides the geopolitics of the region. The US and Cuba are culturally and otherwise so near and yet so far.

As I head home, I cannot shake off the feeling that another Revolution—this time a silent one—is in the offing.

Acknowledgements

I wish to thank the following people for making my journey to Cuba a fruitful experience and helping this book come to life:

In India

- John Brittas, Member of Parliament
- M.A. Baby, CPM Politburo Member and Cubophile
- Alejandro Simancas Marin, former Cuban Ambassador to India
- Abel Aballe Despaigne, deputy head of Mission, Embassy of the Republic of Cuba, New Delhi
- Malena Rojas Medina, secretary, Press and Cultural Affairs, Embassy of the Republic of Cuba, New Delhi
- Karthik Venkatesh, executive editor, Penguin Random House India
- Milee Ashwarya, publisher and senior vice-president, Adult Publishing Group, Penguin India
- Aninda Das and Saloni Mital at Penguin Random House India

In Cuba

- S. Janakiraman, former Indian Ambassador to Cuba
- The Indian embassy in Cuba
- Jessica Guía Valladares, media specialist at the Cuban Ministry of Foreign Affairs (MINREX)

I thank these Cuban officials who took time out from their busy schedules to spend hours with me in Cuba and offer me invaluable insights into how their country is run:

- C. José Ramón Cabañas, former Cuban Ambassador to the US
- Dr Ileana Morales Suárez, director of science and technological innovation at Cuba's Ministry of Public Health
- Santiago Dueñas, director of science and innovation at BioCubaFarma
- Dr Tania Crombet Ramos, clinical research director of the Center of Molecular Immunology (CIM)
- Dr Maria del Carmen Dominguez Horta, head of the Autoimmunity Group at the Center for Genetic Engineering and Biotechnology (CIGB)
- Professor Silvia Odriozola Guitart, dean of the Faculty of Economics at the University of Havana
- Felix Mejinas Ruiz, director, International Relations Department, Havana
- Gihana Galindo Enríquez, commercial head, Cuba's tourism ministry (MINTUR)
- Suyen Rivero Martínez, head of business, MINTUR

- Raul Fornes Valenciano, vice president, National Institute of Sports, Physical Education and Recreation in Cuba

I am deeply indebted to the staff at Havana's iconic Nacional de Cuba Hotel, taxi drivers, guides, men and women on the street, waiters who served me at both private and state-run restaurants and bars in multiple towns, young students, and government officials, some of whom are now trying a hand at entrepreneurship. Foremost among the acquaintances and friendships I made in Havana who played a crucial role in my stay there is my brilliant, young interpreter Gabriela Marrero Martinez.

I wish to acknowledge the people all over the world who are victims of the mindless and brutal sanctions of a few reckless grandees of this world.

I also express my gratitude to:

- The terrific Cuban scholar and author Helen Yaffe at the University of Glasgow for her valuable inputs, and words of caution about missing the woods for the trees
- My paternal uncle Pattiam Rajan, a former member of the Rajya Sabha, for sharing his experience from an official trip he was part of to Cuba in 1978
- My editor at *OPEN*, S. Prasannarajan, for his unstinting support
- My school buddy Byju Sukumaran and friends O.V. Mustafa and Dr Cyriac Joseph whose encouragement steered my writing
- Strategist and former ace foreign correspondent K.P. Nayar for his precious pieces of advice

- Famous and not-so-famous writers from my early teens who stimulated my interest in Cuba
- My siblings Mugdha and Pushyarag
- My wife Aekta Kapoor and daughters Manasvi and Isha
- My mother N.K. Mridula and
- My father Pattiam Gopalan who, over 46 years after his demise, remains my greatest inspiration.

Notes

Reading Fidel in Malayalam

1 'The Soviet Union and the Falklands War', Vojtech Mastny, *Naval War College Review*, Vol. 36, No. 3 (May - June 1983), https://www.jstor.org/stable/44636371?seq=4

2 'Marquez, a household name in Kerala', PTI, 18 April 2014, https://www.business-standard.com/article/pti-stories/marquez-a-household-name-in-kerala-114041800779_1.html

3 'Gone on Gabo', K.P.M. Basheer, The Hindu BusinessLine, 23 April 2014, https://www.thehindubusinessline.com/opinion/gone-on-gabo/article22995170.ece

4 *Fidel Castro Mathathe Patti*, Chintha Publishers; 1989

5 'Christ, Karl Marx and Che: Fidel Castro offers the pope his religious views', Cathy Lynn Grossman, 20 September 2015, https://religionnews.com/2015/09/20/once-catholic-fidel-castro-offers-pope-francis-his-views-on-religion/

6 'Document #15: "History Will Absolve Me," by Fidel Castro (1953)', https://library.brown.edu/create/modernlatinamerica/chapters/chapter-4-cuba/primary-documents-w-accompanying-discussion-

questions/document-no-10-history-will-absolve-me-by-fidel-castro-ruiz/

7   'Fifty years after his death, "Che" Guevara continues to evoke adulation in Kerala', A.S. Jayanth, 9 October 2017, https://www.thehindu.com/news/national/kerala/fifty-years-after-his-death-che-continues-to-inspire-youth/article19824150.ece

8   'Fidel Castro, My Hero in Havana', Ullekh N.P., 2 December 2016, https://openthemagazine.com/features/people/fidel-castro-my-hero-in-havana/

9   Images of Cuba, Gabriel Garcia Marquez, Ocean Press 2017, page 3

10   Soccer in Sun and Shadow, Eduardo Galeano, 2018, Penguin

11   'Fidel Castro, My Hero in Havana', Ullekh N.P., 2 December 2016, https://openthemagazine.com/features/people/fidel-castro-my-hero-in-havana/

12   'Moringa's nutritional value praised in Cuba', 23 November 2023, https://www.plenglish.com/news/2023/11/10/moringas-nutritional-value-praised-in-cuba/

13   The Pyruvate Kinase M1 (PKM1) and PKM2 varieties are high-yielding crops with numerous health benefits. It is even known to suppress the development and progression of prostate cancer. https://www.ncbi.nlm.nih.gov/pmc/articles/PMC9256808/

14   'Kerala and Cuba: Curious twins and winners in public health delivery', Ashok Alexander, 27 June 2018, https://www.livemint.com/Opinion/PNjcw7tBKTF4zvAMu8wK0K/Kerala-and-Cuba-Curious-twins-and-winners-in-public-health.html

Soul-Searching in Cuba

1 'How Far Cry 6 Was Inspired by Cuba's Resolver DIY Philosophy', Joe Rybicki, 13 June 2021, https://news.xbox.com/en-us/2021/06/13/how-far-cry-6-was-inspired-by-cubas-resolver-diy-philosophy/

2 'Why Americans will overpay for Cuba's vintage cars', Belinda Laks, 23 December 2014, https://www.bloomberg.com/news/articles/2014-12-23/cubas-vintage-cars-will-be-costly-for-american-collectors

3 'Over the hump? Cubans hope for end to "camel" buses', Anthony Boadle, 10 August 2007 https://www.reuters.com/article/us-cuba-transport-idUSN3118999320070201/

4 *The Souls of China: The Return of Religion After Mao*, Ian Johnson, Pantheon, 2017

5 'Christianity in China', Eleanor Albert, 11 October 2018, https://www.cfr.org/backgrounder/christianity-china#:~:text=Christianity%20in%20China%20is%20overseen,to%20government%20and%20CCP%20thinking

6 *Cuba: A New History*, Richard Gott, Yale University Press, 2005

7 "Religious Symbolism in Cuban Political Performance', Dr Ivor Miller, *The Drama Review*, 2000, https://muse.jhu.edu/article/33005/summary

8 Ibid.

9 Ibid.

10 'Representing The Revolution: Public History and The Moncada Barracks in Santiago De Cuba', Anita Waters and Luci Fernandes, pp. 125–154, 6 May 2014, https://

www.tandfonline.com/doi/abs/10.1080/08263663.201
2.10817030

11 'Obama and Raúl Castro thank pope for breakthrough
in US-Cuba relations', Dan Roberts and Rory Carroll,
The Guardian, 17 December 2014, https://www.
theguardian.com/world/2014/dec/17/us-cuba-
diplomatic-relations-obama-raul-castro

12 'Factsheet: Santeria in Cuba', United States Commission
for International Religious Freedom, https://www.
uscirf.gov/sites/default/files/2021%20Factsheet%20
-%20Santeria%20in%20Cuba.pdf

Aspiration Nation

1 'Cuba Average Monthly Salary', https://
tradingeconomics.com/cuba/wages

The Sin of Sanctions

1 'Cuba's Ambassador to the United States: Who Is José
Ramón Cabañas Rodríguez?', 25 January 2016, http://
www.allgov.com/news?news=858164

2 'Americans still favor ties with Cuba after Castro's death,
U.S. election', Alex Tyson, 13 December 2016,
https://www.pewresearch.org/short-reads/2016/12/13/
americans-still-favor-ties-with-cuba-after-castros-
death-u-s-election/

3 'Tourism in Cuba', https://www.worlddata.info/america/
cuba/tourism.php

4 'Cuba Seeks to Accelerate Tourism Industry's Recovery',
18 August 2023, https://www.telesurenglish.net/

news/Cuba-Seeks-to-Accelerate-Tourism-Industrys-Recovery-20230818-0006.html

5   https://www.reuters.com/world/americas/cuba-counts-russians-boost-still-ailing-tourism-sector-2024-2024-01-26/

6   'U.S.-Cuban biotech venture created to bring new cancer therapies to USA', Reuters, 26 September 2018, https://www.reuters.com/article/us-cuba-usa-idUSKCN1M62F2/

7   The rapprochement efforts between Cuba and the US, set in motion in 2014-end, were a high point of Obama's foreign policy. But as soon as he became President in 2017, Trump rolled back many historic measures aimed at normalizing relations.

8   'Kennedy Center's Artes De Cuba Festival, An Unprecedented Cultural Bridge, Marisa Arbona-Ruiz, 11 May 2018, https://www.npr.org/sections/altlatino/2018/05/11/610365822/kennedy-centers-artes-de-cuba-festival-an-unprecedented-cultural-bridge

9   'Reagan and Cuba: an analysis of U.S. foreign policy in the 1980s', Wen Wang, September 2021, https://theses.gla.ac.uk/82846/1/2021WangWMRes.pdf

10 'Sen. Rubio denies claims he embellished history', The Associated Press, 21 October 2011, https://www.gainesville.com/story/news/2011/10/21/sen-rubio-denies-claims-he-embellished-history/31820636007/

11 'US Senator Marco Rubio', https://www.rubio.senate.gov/about/

12 'Bombing of Cuban Jetliner: 30 Years Later', 5 October 2016, https://nsarchive2.gwu.edu/NSAEBB/NSAEBB202/index.htm

13 'The 2020 FIU Cuba Poll: How Cuban-Americans in Miami View US Policies Towards Cuba', https://cri.fiu.edu/research/cuba-poll/cuba-poll-2020-powerpoint.pdf

14 '"Havana syndrome" not caused by energy weapon or foreign adversary, intelligence review finds', Shane Harris and John Hudson, *The Washington Post,* 1 March 2023, https://www.washingtonpost.com/national-security/2023/03/01/havana-syndrome-intelligence-report-weapon/

15 'Cuba to Host Secret Chinese Spy Base Focusing on U.S.', Warren P. Strobel and Gordon Lubold, 8 June 2023, https://www.wsj.com/articles/cuba-to-host-secret-chinese-spy-base-focusing-on-u-s-b2fed0e0

16 'Is it time to end the Cuban Embargo?', Gary S. Becker and Richard Posner, 29 January 2015, https://www.chicagobooth.edu/review/is-it-time-to-end-cuban-embargo

17 https://www.becker-posner-blog.com/2014/03/end-the-cuban-embargoposner.html

18 '"We will never negotiate under pressure', ex-Cuba envoy to US says', *MEMO,* Dr Daud Abdullah, 9 April 2023, https://www.middleeastmonitor.com/20230409-we-will-never-negotiate-under-pressure-ex-cuba-envoy-to-us-says/

The Power of BioCubaFarma

1 Access, equity and solidarity: the foundations of Cuba's health system', Outra Saude,14 June 2023, https://peoplesdispatch.org/2023/06/14/access-equity-and-solidarity-the-foundations-of-cubas-health-system/

2   https://www.biocon.com/about-us/our-legacy/
3   'Five Medicines "Made in Cuba" Unique in the World',
     11 December 2018, https://cubaheal.com/2018/12/11/
     five-medicines-made-in-cuba-unique-in-the-world/
4   'Reversing the effects of Alzheimer's Disease: Dr. Ron
     Geyer on NeuroEPO', 23 February 2023,
     https://medicine.usask.ca/news/2023/reversing-
     the-effects-of-alzheimers-disease-dr.-ron-geyer-on-
     neuroepo.php#:~:text=NeuroEPO%2C%20first%20
     developed%20by%20researchers,their%20growth%20
     and%20communication%20mechanisms.
5   Ibid.
6   'UA Health Sciences Researchers Look to Collaborate
     With Cuba on Diabetic Wound Therapy', Rebecca Ruiz
     McGill, 2 March 2016, https://deptmedicine.arizona.
     edu/news/2016/ua-health-sciences-researchers-look-
     collaborate-cuba-diabetic-wound-therapy
7   'Psoriasis – Diagnosis and Treatment', https://cubaheal.
     com/treatment-of-psoriasis/
8   'Comparing the COVID-19 Responses in Cuba and the
     United States', Mary Anne Powell, Paul C Erwin , Pedro
     Mas Bermejo' https://pubmed.ncbi.nlm.nih.gov/34878
     871/#:~:text=Through%20July%2015%2C%202021%
     2C%20the,higher%20in%20the%20United%20States.
9   'Cuba and coronavirus: how Cuban biotech came to
     combat Covid-19', Helen Yaffe, 18 March 2020,
     https://blogs.lse.ac.uk/latamcaribbean/2020/03/18/
     cuba-and-coronavirus-how-cuban-biotech-came-to-
     combat-covid-19/
10   Ibid.

11 'Cuba's contribution to combating Covid-19', Helen Yaffe, 12 March 2020, https://yalebooks.yale.edu/2020/03/12/cubas-contribution-to-combating-covid-19/

12 'Effect of combination of interferon alpha-2b and interferon-gamma or interferon alpha-2b alone for elimination of SARS-CoV-2 viral RNA', R. Pereda et al, June 2020, https://www.medrxiv.org/content/10.1101/2020.05.29.20109199v1

13 Ibid.

14 Ibid.

15 'Therapeutic effectiveness of interferon-alpha 2b against COVID-19: the Cuban experience', R. Pereda et al, https://www.medrxiv.org/content/10.1101/2020.05.29.20109199v1.full.pdf

16 'Cuban drug against coronavirus?', Andreas Knobloch, 4 April 2020, https://www.dw.com/en/cuban-drug-as-possible-treatment-for-coronavirus-patients/a-53015483

17 'Kerala Looks to Buy Cuban "Wonder Drug" Interferon', Ullekh N.P., 10 April 2020, https://openthemagazine.com/features/medicine/kerala-looks-buy-cuban-wonder-drug-interferon/

18 'Why Cuba developed its own Covid vaccine and what happened next', 5 August 2021, https://www.bmj.com/content/374/bmj.n1912#:~:text=Rather%20than%20negotiating%20with%20pharmaceutical,it%20could%20be%20paying%20off.

19 'Cuban Abdala vaccine: Effectiveness in preventing severe disease and death from COVID-19 in Havana,

Cuba; A cohort study', Pedro I. Más-Bermejo et al, https://www.thelancet.com/journals/lanam/article/PIIS2667-193X(22)00183-1/fulltext

20 'Unexpected Cuba', Emily Morris, *New Left Review*, July-August 2014, https://newleftreview.org/issues/ii88/articles/emily-morris-unexpected-cuba

21 'The Cuban connection: India & Cuba forge a strong bond', Dr Aparaajita Pandey, 2 June 2023, https://www.financialexpress.com/business/defence-the-cuban-connection-india-cuba-forge-a-strong-bond-3111598/

22 'Noam Chomsky on Academic Freedom and Intellectual Dissent', 19 July 2021, https://allea.org/noam-chomsky-on-academic-freedom-and-intellectual-dissent/

Healers of Our Age

1 'The Health System in Cuba: Origin, Doctrine and Results', Salim Lamrani, 7 July 2021, https://journals.openedition.org/etudescaribeennes/24110

2 Ibid.

3 'Physicians Density', https://www.cia.gov/the-world-factbook/field/physicians-density/

4 'Rapid Response to "Planning the healthcare workforce: how many GPs do we need?"', https://www.bmj.com/content/376/bmj.o123/rr-5#:~:text=Cuba%20has%20almost%2050%2C000%20medical,the%20world%20in%20this%20sector.

5 'Cuban Medical Internationalism: A Paradigm for South-South Co-operation', Helen Yaffe, 11 December 2023, https://www.scienceopen.com/hosted-document?doi=10.13169/intejcubastud.15.2.0203

6 'The Health System in Cuba: Origin, Doctrine and Results', Salim Lamrani, 7 July 2021, https://journals.openedition.org/etudescaribeennes/24110

7 'We Should Applaud the Cuban Health System—and Learn From It', Medea Benjamin, 22 April 2020, https://jacobin.com/2020/04/cuba-healthcare-coronavirus

8 'How much does Taiwan depend on China?', Thomas Kohlmann, 8 June 2022, https://www.dw.com/en/how-much-does-taiwan-depend-on-china/a-62725691#:~:text=But%2C%20while%20the%202021%20gross,from%20the%20International%20Monetary%20Fund

9 'Cross Strait Relations', https://www.taiwan.gov.tw/content_6.php#:~:text=Today%2C%20Taiwan%20is%20one%20of,trade%20was%20US%24273.06%20billion.

10 'Is it time to end the Cuban Embargo?', Gary S. Becker and Richard Posner, 29 January 2015, https://www.chicagobooth.edu/review/is-it-time-to-end-cuban-embargo

11 'Michael Parenti on the Cuban Revolution', https://www.youtube.com/watch?v=npkeecCErQc

12 'Cuba says nearly all its doctors have returned from Brazil', 21 December 2018, https://www.reuters.com/article/world/cuba-says-nearly-all-its-doctors-have-returned-from-brazil-idUSKCN1OK213/

13 'The Health System in Cuba: Origin, Doctrine and Results', Salim Lamrani, 7 July 2021, https://journals.openedition.org/etudescaribeennes/24110

14 'Responses to the Covid 19 pandemic: What Kerala did differently', Energy News Monitor, 27 August 2021,

https://www.orfonline.org/expert-speak/responses-to-the-covid-19-pandemic-what-kerala-did-differently

15 'How Solidarity is Controlling Contagion in Kerala', Prerna Singh, 8 June 2020, https://casi.sas.upenn.edu/iit/prernasingh

16 Ibid.

17 'At 4x of national average, Kerala health is highest in India', Preetu Nair, 14 September 2022, https://timesofindia.indiatimes.com/india/at-4x-of-national-average-kerala-health-spend-is-highest-in-india/articleshow/94186793.cms?utm_source=contentofinterest&utm_medium=text&utm_campaign=cppst&pcode=461

18 'Re-engineering primary healthcare in Kerala, A. Krishnan et al, 21 March 2023, https://www.ncbi.nlm.nih.gov/pmc/articles/PMC9983803/

19 'Strategies and challenges in Kerala's response to the initial phase of COVID-19 pandemic: a qualitative descriptive study', Kannamkottapilly Chandrasekharan Prajitha et al, 14 March 2022, https://pubmed.ncbi.nlm.nih.gov/34244285/

20 'NCDC hails Kerala for its success in checking Nipah spread', The Hindu Bureau, 8 October 2023, https://www.thehindu.com/news/national/kerala/ncdc-hails-kerala-for-its-success-in-checking-nipah-spread/article67393780.ece

21 'Kerala, Cuba to join hands to share health-care expertise: CM', 16 June 2023, https://www.thehindu.com/news/national/kerala/kerala-cuba-to-join-hands-to-share-health-care-expertise-cm/article66977471.ece

22 'Access, equity and solidarity: the foundations of Cuba's health system', Outra Saude, 14 June 2023, https://

peoplesdispatch.org/2023/06/14/access-equity-and-solidarity-the-foundations-of-cubas-health-system/

23 https://www.semanticscholar.org/paper/Cuban-Medical-Internationalism%3A-A-Paradigm-for-Yaffe/e13898c36b6d9490e5109ed32fe748f4cba0d817

24 'Cuba has a history of sending medical teams to nations in crisis', Mariya Petkova, 1 May 2020, https://www.aljazeera.com/features/2020/4/1/cuba-has-a-history-of-sending-medical-teams-to-nations-in-crisis

Breaking With the Past

1 'War Communism', https://www.britannica.com/money/War-Communism

2 'Lenin's New Economic Policy: What it was and how it Changed the Soviet Union', Helene M. Glaza, 2009, Vol 1., no. 11, http://www.inquiriesjournal.com/articles/1670/lenins-new-economic-policy-what-it-was-and-how-it-changed-the-soviet-union

3 'Mipymes: New Private Economic Actors in Cuba and the Challenge for a Feasible Socialism', Gina Mardones Loncomilla, 16 April 2023, https://link.springer.com/chapter/10.1007/978-3-031-29129-6_11#Abs1

4 'Proceedings of the 2019 International Conference on Management, Education Technology and Economics (ICMETE 2019)', https://www.atlantis-press.com/proceedings/icmete-19/125908380

5 'New Yorkers in Need: A Look at Poverty Trends in New York State in the Last Decade', December 2022,

https://www.osc.ny.gov/reports/new-yorkers-need-look-poverty-trends-new-york-state-last-decade

6   'In order to understand the brutality of American capitalism, you have to start on the plantation', Matthew Desmond, 14 August 2019, https://www.nytimes.com/interactive/2019/08/14/magazine/slavery-capitalism.html

7   https://nysiaf.org/the-8-biggest-challenges-facing-immigrants/

8   'As Cuba's private sector roars back, choices and inequality rise', Ed Augustin, 19 July 2023, https://www.aljazeera.com/economy/2023/7/19/as-cubas-private-sector-roars-back-choices-and-inequality-rise

9   'Party and State in China', Nathan Sperber, *New Left Review* (July-August 2023), https://newleftreview.org/issues/ii142/articles/nathan-sperber-party-and-state-in-china

Vitamin R in Tobacco Land

1   'They love their job, reading to cigar workers in Cuba', Associated Press, 3 July 2021, https://www.nbcnews.com/news/latino/love-job-reading-cigar-workers-cuba-rcna1335

Che Guevara's Undying Spell

1   *Che Guevara: The Economics of Revolution*, Dr Helen Yaffe, Basingstoke, UK; Palgrave Macmillan, 2009

2 'Che Guevara: The Economics of Revolution', Helen Yaffe, 23 June 2009, https://palgrave.typepad.com/yaffe/page/11/

3 The Fall of Che Guevara and the Changing Face of the Cuban Revolution', 18 October 1965, https://www.cia.gov/readingroom/docs/CIA-RDP79T00472A000800020004-5.pdf

4 'Che Guevara on Africa (Interview with Josie Fanon', 26 January 2021, https://priyavprabhakar.medium.com/che-guevara-on-africa-interview-with-josie-fanon-1aefc395fdfb

Hardships of a Small Neighbour

1 'The Entrepreneurs Transforming Cuba', Belly of the Beast Cuba, https://www.youtube.com/watch?v=OQ_1uXKFhWo&t=4s

2 'Cuban entrepreneurs get business training from the US, and hope that Biden lifts sanctions', Andrea Rodriguez, 27 June 2023, https://apnews.com/article/cuba-small-businesses-private-enterprise-8301fd145b2ceece20d2bc618551345e

3 'As Cuba's private sector grows, entrepreneurs get a warm welcome in Miami', Carmen Sesin and Orlando Matos, 5 October 2023, https://www.nbcnews.com/news/latino/cuba-private-sector-entrepreneurs-attend-miami-conference-rcna118932

4 Ibid.

5 'Trump applied in 2008 to register his trademark in Cuba: report', John Bowden, 22 September 2020, https://

thehill.com/policy/international/americas/517537-trump-applied-in-2008-to-register-his-trademark-in-cuba-report/

6   'Trump registered his trademark in Cuba in 2008 to build hotels, casinos and golf courses', Nora Gamez Torres, 22 September 2020, https://www.miamiherald.com/news/nation-world/world/americas/cuba/article245902870.html#storylink=cpyhttps://www.miamiherald.com/news/nation-world/world/americas/cuba/article245902870.html

7   'Exiles in America Soften Stance on Cuba Ties', Adalberto Toque, 13 March 2014, https://www.nbcnews.com/news/latino/exiles-america-soften-stance-cuba-ties-n44121

8   'You Were Lied to About Cuba Socialism', BreakThrough News, 25 May 2022, https://www.youtube.com/watch?v=Faj8EM59xOs

9   Rolling Stones Thrill Huge Crowd at Historic Havana Show, 26 March 2016, Richard L. Dewey, https://www.rollingstone.com/music/music-live-reviews/rolling-stones-thrill-huge-crowd-at-historic-havana-show-160574/

10 'Rep. Jim McGovern: Our Cuba Policy is an "Embarrassment"', Belly of the Beast Cuba, https://www.youtube.com/watch?v=sjblEqqddlg&t=32s

11 Using Cuba's Protests as a Chance to Denounce the Left', Aviva Chomsky, 19 August 2021, https://nacla.org/news/2021/08/17/cuba-protests-left

12 'U.S. Boycotts Cuban Baseball Team's Integration in WBC', 7 December 2022,

http://www.periodico26.cu/index.php/en/cuba-news-2/11076-u-s-boycotts-cuban-baseball-team-s-integration-in-wbc

Resistance and Transition

1 *Cuba: An American History*, Ada Ferrer, Simon and Schuster, 2022
2 Ibid.
3 Ibid.
4 Ibid.
5 Williams makes this observation in a write-up titled *Contested Narratives: South African and Cuban Military Action in Angola (1987–1988)*
6 'Nelson Mandela on How Cuba "Destroyed the Myth of the Invincibility of the White Oppressor"', 11 December 2013, https://www.democracynow.org/2013/12/11/nelson_mandela_on_how_cuba_destroyed
7 'As independent media blossoms in Cuba, journalists face a crackdown', Ed Augustin, 20 January 2023, *The Guardian*, https://www.theguardian.com/world/2023/jan/20/independent-media-cuba-journalists-crackdown
8 'Fidel Castro's "most difficult interview"', https://www.youtube.com/watch?v=39o2QtloOgI
9 *What I Learned About Cuba by Going to Cuba*, Antonio R. Zamora, Cuba Libre Publications, Miami, 2013
10 'In 1985 interview, Castro spoke of fearing U.S. invasion', https://www.youtube.com/watch?v=xxbGh_1VFsY

11 'The papal visit that changed Cuba', Narda Baeza Bickel, 21 September 2015, https://news.umich.edu/the-papal-visit-that-changed-cuba/

12 'The Strategic Importance of Cuba', Emanuel Pietrobon, 8 November 2023, https://valdaiclub.com/a/highlights/the-strategic-importance-of-cuba/

Scan QR code to access the
Penguin Random House India website